The Emergence of God

A Rationalist Jewish Exploration of Divine Consciousness

David W. Nelson

University Press of America,® Inc.
Lanham • Boulder • New York • Toronto • Plymouth, UK

Copyright © 2015 by University Press of America,® Inc.
4501 Forbes Boulevard, Suite 200, Lanham, Maryland 20706
UPA Acquisitions Department (301) 459-3366

Unit A, Whitacre Mews, 26-34 Stannary Street,
London SE11 4AB, United Kingdom

All rights reserved

British Library Cataloguing in Publication Information Available

Library of Congress Control Number: 2015933171
ISBN: 978-0-7618-6582-7 (pbk : alk. paper)—ISBN: 978-0-7618-6583-4 (electronic)

Contents

Preface		v
1	In Search of God's Consciousness	1
2	The Brain, The Mind, and Consciousness	17
3	The Emergence of God	37
4	Emergent God and Mitzvot/Commandments	61
5	Scrutinizing the Model	95
6	The Ultimate Mitzvah	119
7	Exploring Loneliness	141
Epilogue: A Brief, Final Thought: But What If I'm Wrong?		153

Preface

Some years ago, I organized and taught a monthly Torah study group for the board members of a local Jewish organization. During our first session, one gentleman said, with a combination of frustration and mischievous humor, "I just don't get the God thing." He was intrigued by the biblical narrative and delighted with the wide-ranging discussions that flowed from it, but the whole notion of a controlling, sentient, puppet-master God just didn't sit right with him. His discomfort became an ongoing theme in all future study sessions.

Although that student was particularly amusing in the way he expressed his theological perplexity, he was neither the first nor the last to harbor such sentiments. In fact, I believe that a great many contemporary American Jews—most especially those who do not identify themselves as Orthodox—do not get the God thing. Some cope with these feelings by vigorously proclaiming themselves to be atheists, taking their cues from thinkers and authors such as Richard Dawkins, Christopher Hitchens, and the like. They lead "culturally Jewish" lives and engage in ritual, celebration, and observance with a constant, conscious sense that these behaviors have nothing whatsoever to do with God. Others take a more moderate approach and use the language of God as it occurs throughout Jewish life without ever taking it seriously. They say the words because the tradition prescribes that they do so, but their recitation has no meaning for them.

For close to two decades, I have been trying to find ways to help these two Jewish groups think creatively and innovatively about God. In the first stage, I explored new God metaphors—that is to say, new ways of speaking, and therefore of thinking, about God—that I drew from the vocabulary of modern physics. The result was a deep sense of reverence for God redefined as the creative and generative powers of nature. But that result still left God without personality, without mind, and without the ability to interact.

My dissatisfaction with that result led me to this book, my second stage. In the pages that follow, I have searched for a path by which modern, liberal, scientifically minded individuals might understand God without being forced to profess things that they "just don't get." I have little doubt that my journey has not yet ended, and that there will be more stages as I continue to think seriously about God, human beings, and the continuing struggle that binds them together. Such thinking, in the end, is what Jewish life is all about.

The process of writing a book like this involves many, many hours of solitary thinking, imagining, writing, and revising. But those hours could never take place without the encouragement, support, and assistance of close friends and caring colleagues. I am particularly grateful to my colleagues at Bard College, most especially Professors Jacob Neusner and Bruce Chilton. The friendship and support from Professor Gary Kates of Pomona College spurred me to think critically at many points along the way. Advice and resources came often and willingly from Professor David Kraemer of the Jewish Theological Seminary of America. And the courage to think in new directions that I received from Rabbi Irving "Yitz" Greenberg during my many years working at CLAL (the National Jewish Center for Learning and Leadership) inspired me profoundly. My editor Eliot Werner was of immeasurable assistance, not only in his gentle suggestions for improving my writing, but in his willingness to work with me under a very tight deadline. And Rabbi Randy Kafka's careful reading of the entire manuscript was an enormous help to me. Finally, my thanks and love go always to Rachel, Lev, Adin, and Ziv for their constant support, encouragement, and love. They are the very best of what a family can be.

Chapter One

In Search of God's Consciousness

AN UNSATISFYING CONCLUSION

In 2005 my book *Judaism, Physics and God: Searching for Sacred Metaphors in a Post-Einstein World* was published. The process of writing it was fascinating to me in many ways. Most significantly was that despite my initial plan for the book, I ended up going to unexpected places. Chief among those places was the development and articulation of my own belief in a nonpersonal God.

Over the course of my reading, thinking, and writing, I came to the conclusion that I *do* believe in God, but that the God in which I believe is *not* the personal (that is, person-like) deity described by most of our ancient Jewish metaphors. Those metaphors—including Father, King, Shepherd, Man-of-War, friend, husband, lover, and teacher—all suggest a person, or at the very least a being who functions much like a person. In colloquial parlance this is the image of the "old man with the white beard" (although it is not clear to me exactly why so many people are simultaneously taken with and repelled by that particular description). Instead of all this, I believe in a God who is the sum total of the organizational forces in the universe, the natural powers and laws that give structure, beauty, and elegance to the universe on every level, from the subatomic to the super-galactic. These forces are at the very heart of creation—that is, of the process whereby the universe went from an unimaginably tiny spot of immense energy (the Big Bang) to the vast, complex thing it is today in under 15 billion years. They are forces that, with a single exception (the behavior of extremely tiny things, as defined by quantum mechanics), argue powerfully that there is no randomness in the universe. The universe is *not* random. It is organized and structured. And it is in this organization and structure, in this nearly total lack of randomness, that God appears. God is the forces of organization, structure, and—although the word is perhaps a bit less at home in the world of science than in that of art or aesthetics—*beauty* that have given rise to our universe and that continue to guide its behavior and evolution. In the words of the traditional Jewish morning service, God is the one who "renews the act of creation every day, in goodness."[1]

Biophysicist Harold Morowitz summarizes the situation nicely:

> This God of natural law or the God of Reason is an immanent God, mysterious and probably impenetrable or unknowable. This pantheistic view provides a context within which the study of the laws of nature rises to a religious undertaking, an attempt to know the mind of God. In such a context, science is a vocation. However, this God of the laboratory and observatory is cold and distant and listens to no one's prayers. But according to Spinoza, he may and should be adored. To some this seems a contradiction. Lacking the emotional impact of traditional Western religion, it seems quite unsatisfactory for the religion of the people.[2]

Part of the reason this way of thinking about God seems "quite unsatisfactory for the religion of the people" is that it undermines the traditional notion that imagines an Intelligence—that is, a conscious, thinking, planning Being, a Great *Someone* who existed before the universe and independently of it. The natural forces that give structure to reality do not think or imagine or plan. They are simply principles of nature,[3] inherent to the fabric of reality in this universe. This is not always clear from the way we use language. For example, toward the end of a cloudy day I might remark, "The sun is trying to break through!" My imprecise, metaphorical language, which personifies the sun, suggests that the sun is a conscious being that has will and desire. In fact, the sun is merely a star, an inanimate astronomical body. My comment is a quirk of human language and thought, not intended to be taken precisely. Even casual scientific language often engages in such misleading figures of speech, as in "Nature abhors a vacuum" and "Water seeks its own level."

By the time I had finished writing *Judaism, Physics and God*, my belief in a nonpersonal God had become clear in my own mind. It did not make me uncomfortable. It felt right. But it left me a bit unsatisfied, as one might feel after finishing a meal that fulfilled basic nutritional needs but left the diners wanting something more substantial. A large number of the fundamental assumptions of Jewish tradition seem to rest on belief in a personal God: the notion that God cares, loves us, chose us as a people, brought us out of Egyptian slavery, gave us laws, and intervened (and intervenes) in our history are just a few. Prayer, while not impossible by any means, is harder to understand and to engage in if one rejects a personal sense of God. And the system of *mitzvot*, religious obligations incumbent upon us because they were "commanded by God," must be radically redefined.

These issues in no way constituted fatal flaws in my belief in God-as-the-principles-of-nature. But over time I found myself focusing more and more on Morowitz's indictment of my view of God as "quite unsatisfactory for the religion of the people." I began to dwell on the question of whether there could be any room in my personal beliefs for a sense of a God who was aware, had feelings, and could interact. In other words, I began to wonder whether I could find any path that would lead me to a sense that God—as I had come to imagine God—could be "conscious." The force of gravity, defined by Einstein as the curvature of spacetime, is no more conscious than the stone upon which it acts when the stone rolls down a mountainside. Likewise, the Big Bang (and the subatomic processes that govern how the "stuff" of the universe behaves) have no awareness and cannot remember, love, or be angry. But was there any way for me to imagine a conscious God? My basic beliefs would seem to have left me no room for such an entity, but I needed to try to find it. The search is at the heart of this book. But first, some caveats.

METAPHOR AND THE THING ITSELF

Throughout *Judaism, Physics and God*, I was careful to speak about *metaphors* for God. I started with the premise that all God language is, by its nature, metaphorical. I explored and critiqued traditional metaphors for God and proposed and critiqued new metaphors drawn from the conceptual vocabulary of physics. Following (humbly) in the footsteps of the great twelfth century philosopher Moses Maimonides, I drew a clear and careful distinction between the metaphors that we use in speaking about God and God's true self. In other words, I was not talking about what God actually is—for, according to Maimonides, we can know nothing of that. Rather, I was talking about the language we use to suggest some of the things we believe about God. At one point I even quoted Professor Neil Gillman as cautioning that we must not get confused between a metaphor for a thing and the thing itself. A metaphor is suggestive and impressionistic, not precise and descriptive. One of my favorite examples is the language of Psalm 23: "Adonai is my Shepherd." By these words the psalmist wishes to convey his belief that God cares for us, protects and sustains us, guides us in our lives, and so on. It does *not* follow, as it would if "shepherd" were a true description of the thing itself rather than a metaphor, that God occasionally takes one of us home, slaughters us, and feeds us to His family for dinner! It's *only* a metaphor and metaphors are not meant to be taken literally. This somewhat obvious point was the basis for my claim that God as the Big Bang, or God as fractal-shaped, were metaphors that could stand next to God as King or God as Father.

As I began to think more about whether God could be thought of as conscious, a strange thing happened. One day a close friend, Professor Gary Kates of Pomona College, challenged me: Was I still speaking about God metaphors, or was I now speaking about God, really and actually, the thing itself? I began to respond, almost as a reflex, that of course I was only speaking metaphorically, but then I caught myself. I was no longer sure. Perhaps, in fact, I had gradually left behind the comfort zone of metaphor. I call it a "comfort zone" because we can speak metaphorically about things without risking too much, and without getting into too much trouble. ("Oh well, it's *only* a metaphor!") At this point in my thinking, I am moving beyond the strict confines of metaphor and have begun to think of this work as the development of a *theory* of God. Theories are systems or models that are constructed in order to explain the observed data. They do not claim to be the last word on a topic, but only to be what their proponents feel is the best explanation for all the data. They may be supported by further thought and research, or they may be challenged by different theories that explain the data in a better way. What I am proposing in these pages, then, is a model that seems to me to explain how the world works, or—to be a bit more blunt— how *God* works in and with the world.

SCIENCE AND BELIEF

I have often suggested that rather than seeing science and religion as competitors in a zero-sum game, in which a win by one must entail the defeat of the other, it would be more interesting to ask how the insights of the one (science) might inform the thinking of the other (religion). But in the pages that follow, I shall be much less cautious, much more bold and audacious (in other words, more *chutzpah-dik*). I am suggesting that we apply *scientific thinking* or the *scientific method* to religion. A typical definition of the scientific method is this:

> The principles and empirical processes of discovery and demonstration considered characteristic of or necessary for scientific investigation, generally involving the observation of phenomena, the formulation of a hypothesis concerning the phenomena, experimentation to demonstrate the truth or falseness of the hypothesis, and a conclusion that validates or modifies the hypothesis.[4]

The critical part of this definition is that the process begins with "observation of phenomena." Observation becomes the basis for conclusions about the way things are. This process seems quite simple; it is, after all, the way we approach the world. For example, if I wake up in the morning, look out the window, and see a gray sky, and then I notice dark clouds forming on the western edge of the horizon and I see that the barometric pressure—as indicated by the barometer mounted on my wall—is dropping, and I turn on the news and hear a weather forecast for intermittent rain showers today, I take all these observations together and conclude that it may very well rain in the coming hours. Such conclusions based on observation and analysis of data do not seem revolutionary. We function like this many times a day, without even paying attention to the fact.

But this is *not* the way Western revealed religion has typically functioned. Rather, the truths of religion, at least in the form best known to most of us, are revealed truths—that is, truths that are believed to have come to someone (often a prophet) directly from God, without the prophet having to go through the usual process of observing the phenomena of the world, analyzing them, and coming to conclusions. In the context of religious faith, this approach makes sense. After all, classical Jewish tradition claims God to be the omniscient and omnipotent source of truth.[5] And even the most arrogant scientist will not claim that his or her theory is Absolutely True, but only that it seems the best explanation for all the data up to this point. So if we have to choose between Truth delivered to us neatly packaged and absolutely certain from a source that by definition is omniscient and perfect, and the scientific method (which requires years of hard work, careful thought, tuition payments, and no ultimate guarantee of success), it makes perfect sense to choose revelation. The problem is that at several points in human history, and overwhelmingly since the Enlightenment, Western civilization has not trusted anything we could not prove using our minds. So even though the promise of revealed truth seems awfully tempting, it is often declined in the modern era because we can't be *really* sure that these prepackaged truths are in fact true. At least with the scientific method I have to show you all the steps in my research and thinking, and you have the opportunity to question the thought process—or even to replicate my research procedures in your own lab—to make sure that my observed results come out the same for you. With revealed truth there are no steps in the process. A prophet goes up to a mountain, or out into a desert, and comes back bearing New Revealed Perfect Truth. Take it or leave it.

Although I am not a scientist, I believe in the scientific method. I do not accept most of the revealed truths of Jewish tradition. The fact that ancient texts—texts, by the way, that I value and cherish immensely—tell me that such-and-such is the case does *not* lead me to believe such-and-such, especially if the claim is not borne out, or (worse yet) is contradicted, by our observations of the world. I believe in the extraordinary power of the human mind to formulate penetrating questions and try to answer them. I do *not* believe that we will eventually know everything. The limits on our knowledge and understanding, however, do not bar us from asking questions and trying to figure things out. Asking questions and seeking truth, even when we have a suspicion that the entire truth may not ultimately be accessible to us, is part and parcel of our humanness. Because of my deep belief in the power of the human mind to seek truth by observing, analyzing, and reasoning, that is how I must go about my search for a conscious God.

THE ROAD AHEAD

The purpose of this book is to explore the phenomenon of consciousness, try to figure out whether and how we may properly speak of God as being conscious, and try to fit all of this into a more-or-less coherent and comprehensive vision of Jewish life, Jewish thought, and Jewish belief. In doing so, I face a methodological concern. In *Judaism, Physics and God,* I was faced with a serious challenge—namely, how I, a rabbi with no post-high school academic training in science, would learn enough physics to be able to write intelligently about physics and Judaism. But I read a few dozen good books by well-known physicists who delight in sharing their expertise with a non-expert, nontechnical, and mathematically challenged audience, and eventually I learned the basic concepts. As I read, I developed a broad (if somewhat oversimplified and nontechnical) sense of the state of the art in physics. In the current project, alas, things are not so easy. In physics the basic ideas of cosmology, quantum theory, general and special relativity, and chaos theory are pretty well agreed upon by physicists. Of the topics I addressed in my physics work, only string theory remains a controversial work in progress, and there I was forced to rely on just one author (Professor Brian Greene of Columbia University), mostly because he was the only one who had written on string theory for a general audience. I completely avoided some of the biggest questions currently being debated by physicists—namely, the existence and influence of dark energy and dark matter—for there were no explanations of these issues that were accessible to the nontechnical reader.

With the study of consciousness, however, the situation is different. The whole field, known generally as cognitive science, is in its infancy. When I was an undergraduate (in the early 1970s), we did not even have a cognitive science department. The combination of neuroscience, computer science, artificial intelligence, cognitive psychology and neuropsychology, and other related areas that make up the field is so new—and in such an early evolutionary stage—that it is impossible to read a small number of good books and find consensus about the basic truths of the field. This newness is starkly described by Jeff Hawkins, a highly respected entrepreneur, computer scientist, and engineer. In the introduction to his book *On Intelligence,* he writes:

> When I first became interested in brains many years ago,[6] I went to my local library to look for a good book that would explain how brains worked. . . . There were books on relativity theory, black holes, magic, and mathematics—whatever I was fascinated with at the moment. Yet my search for a satisfying

brain book turned up empty. I came to realize that no one had any idea how the brain actually worked. There weren't even any bad or unproven theories; there simply were none.[7]

In the thirty-plus years since Hawkins's original search, many books have been published. But in this brand new field, there is nothing like a consensus about the basic ideas. This leaves me, a nonexpert trying to acquire some basic knowledge, with a dilemma. How will I know when I have read "the" definitive expert treatment of the topic? For that matter, how will I know when the book I have innocently read is—in the opinion of most experts— sheer nonsense, dreamed up by some author whom no one in the field respects? These and similar questions fill me with trepidation but do not stop my curiosity. So I plunge ahead, aware of the dangers, constantly reading new books, and relying on the kind assistance of friends and acquaintances who *are* credentialed, academic experts in the field to keep me out of the worst trouble.

WHAT IS CONSCIOUSNESS?

The phenomenon of consciousness is at once deeply and thoroughly mysterious and as commonplace and familiar as breathing. In using the word "consciousness," I am not referring here to the mystical and profound consciousness that we often imagine to be the spiritual state of Buddhist monks or kabbalistic *rebbes*. That sort of consciousness is exotic and exciting, but it is not my focus. Rather, I am referring to the garden-variety consciousness that every single human being experiences every waking hour of every day (and perhaps some of the sleeping hours as well—but that only complicates the question more!). This sort of everyday consciousness is another word for awareness.

Consider the following completely ordinary description: I leave my house on a typical weekday morning, on my way to work. As I walk down the driveway, I glance at my watch to see exactly how many minutes I have to get the shuttle bus on the corner; if it's at least three minutes I can walk at a leisurely pace, but less than two means I have to half-jog. On the road I am constantly looking out for cars that zoom down our country road at 55 miles per hour. As I walk, I notice how fresh everything smells after last night's rain, and pat my pockets to be sure I have my phone, wallet, and keys, at the same time that I'm going over my schedule in my head. I have meetings scheduled with two students before I teach. I remember that I didn't finish composing homework sentences for my Hebrew students, and I start composing them mentally. When I get to the bus stop, I'll write them down. As I walk—always moving quickly—I begin to get too warm, so I unzip my jacket. I get to the bus stop and see that there are three students waiting there.

I have to figure out as I get close if they are students I know (should I say hello?) and if they are plugged in to their music (in which case they won't hear my hello). It occurs to me that I left the outgoing mail on the kitchen table instead of bringing it with me to drop in the mailbox. Another glance at my watch: no time to run back and get it. And I am always singing or humming songs in my head.

This brief and rather incomplete portrait of my state of mind during four or five minutes of a typical weekday morning is remarkable in two ways. First of all, it is remarkable in its utter ordinariness. It is so completely mundane, so absolutely unremarkable! Any of us could write such a description of a five-minute stretch of typical time in a typical day. But why would we? It's so un-noteworthy! But the second, truly remarkable thing about my description is that it *is* so ordinary. I don't have to work at it. It is not mentally taxing to notice traffic and my watch and the feel of my cellphone in my pocket and the students waiting for the bus and the Beatles song in my head and all the other pieces of my surroundings that I process. Such "situational awareness" is the normal, unremarkable state of the human being. We are conscious of dozens, perhaps even hundreds, of things at every moment.

This consciousness consists of two basic categories of stuff. One category includes awareness of external elements of our physical surroundings. Those don't seem terribly mysterious to us on a day-to-day basis. We simply take for granted the sensory inputs of our eyes, ears, noses, and kinesthetic senses (and, somewhat less often, our sense of taste). We assume that there is nothing special about the fact that we notice traffic noises, the colors and textures of the things we see, the smells that constantly bombard our noses, the feelings of gravel crunching underfoot, and so on. A subcategory consists of our monitoring of internal sensations. Our stomachs grumble, reminding us that we are hungry. We experience headaches, sore muscles, or the wonderful relief from a minor injury that has finally healed. We feel hot or cold or comfortable.

This constant awareness of the sensory inputs of our surroundings and the internal state of our bodies is a marvelous thing when we pay attention to it. How do we distinguish between the feel of a cellphone and a wallet in a pocket? And what exactly is involved in the perception of the redness of that red sweater? And how do we keep track of so very many inputs at once? No engineer or computer architect has succeeded in building a machine that can sense, process, and keep track of so many inputs simultaneously—yet we do it without a moment's thought. It is utterly natural and effortless.

The second category of stuff that inhabits (or "clutters") our daily consciousness is mental. There's the song I keep singing "in my head"—that is to say, I am not singing aloud or even mouthing the words, but the words and melody are there, playing "in my head." There's the internal dialogue that we carry on with ourselves, about little things and big things, decisions that must be made or plans for the day. We all talk with ourselves all the time. And we do it without making a sound, without moving our lips. We also have a constant stream of thoughts. I'm not talking about Big Ideas here, like relativity or theology or the latest world-shattering crisis in the morning news. I'm talking about little thoughts—mental Post-Its that we constantly stick up on our brains. I must remember to call those friends to find out if they want to come over for a Scrabble game this weekend. I never replied to that email from a student who wanted to make an appointment with me. I have a book on my desk that needs to be returned to the library. These little thoughts constantly run through our heads.

Again, the catalogue of internal consciousness could go on endlessly but the point is simple: These thoughts, songs, internal dialogues, and the like are so natural, so completely ordinary, that we pay no attention to them. We are not surprised by them. Indeed, if I woke up one morning and found that they were gone, that I did *not* have these little mental happenings going on, that my brain was "quiet," I think it would be terrifying. Like sudden blindness or deafness, but far worse.

But if we think about this internal mental clutter, several questions beg to be addressed. First of all, where is it happening? Two paragraphs back I used the phrase "in my head" and put it in quotation marks. Why the quotation marks? Because although we *assume* that this stuff is happening in our heads, there's no real sensation that it's there. When I have a pebble in my shoe, I *feel* the pain *in* my foot. When I have a mosquito bite on my wrist, I feel it there. If I have an upset stomach, I feel it there. The doctor asks me, "Where does it hurt?" and I can answer. But aside from occasional headaches, we do not *feel* that anything else happens in our heads. Instead we have all accepted the notion—rather uncritically and unquestioningly—that mental awareness and mental processes happen in our brains, which are located in our heads. But if we were never told that thoughts, memories, sensations, daydreams, and emotions happen in our heads, would we know it? Would we intuit it? I don't think so.

In fact, this nonintuitive assumption about where mental activity takes place is unique to our modern era. In ancient times the notion of where "self" happens involved more visceral parts of our anatomy. When the biblical prophet Jeremiah is in existential agony, torn between his desire not to prophesy on the one hand (because prophesying about the utter corruption of the society in which one lives can make one's life pretty awful) and his compulsion to do so on the other, he says, "My guts, my guts, I writhe! Oh, the walls of my heart—my heart moans within me, I cannot be silent."[8] This sense of the physical locale of emotions is consistent with experience. When we feel emotionally agitated, we sense a churning in our bellies and an acceleration of our heartbeat. Based on these sensations, it makes perfect sense that in the traditional liturgy of Yom Kippur, when the text describes

God's knowledge of all matters (even those we keep secretly locked inside ourselves), it says, "You search out all the chambers of the belly and investigate the kidneys and the heart."[9] Even prayer book translations that are often slavishly literal understand the intention of this anatomical specificity. The old *High Holiday Prayer Book* of the Conservative movement renders the passage, "Thou searchest out the heart of man, and probest all our thoughts and aspirations,"[10] and an ArtScroll version translates it as "You probe all innermost chambers and test thoughts and emotions."[11] These ancient expressions of the location of emotion, thought, and conscience seem somewhat quaint to us, now that we are armed with a relatively sophisticated sense of physiology and we know the functions of heart, kidneys, intestines, and stomach. But they made sense in the ancient world because those parts of our bodies are indeed where we *feel* strong emotions.

Notwithstanding the clarity with which we feel love, anger, frustration, nervousness, fear, or calm in the core of our bodies, modern science tells us unequivocally that consciousness takes place in our brains—that is, in our heads. This observation leads to an important insight: even though our consciousness is completely natural and automatic, like our breathing or our heartbeat, its primary function (that is, awareness) is not immediately or easily comprehensible to us. Somewhat counterintuitively, it is not so easy for us to reflect upon, or be aware of, our awareness.

When we *do* pay attention to our awareness, we find that being conscious might be described as "what it is like to be me." In other words, when I use the first-person singular pronouns "I" or "me," what I am referring to is what I experience to be myself. This is a complex of ideas, sensations, memories, feelings, and much more, contained in a body[12] that I identify, perceive, and think of as Me. One of the many curious aspects of this universal experience is that although I know and understand a tremendous amount about what it is like to be Me, I know very little about what it is like to be someone else. Think about it. Every single moment of every single day, I experience myself, often in relationship to other people. I assume intuitively that they experience their selves in the same way—or nearly the same way—as I do. But in fact, when I give it some thought, I have no real sense of what it would be like to be someone else! The attempt to understand this process is made regularly by actors, whose job it is to "be" (or, more precisely, to pretend to be) someone else for the duration of a play or a movie. But the actor's job is really only to *behave* like someone else. Some actors may talk about the need to "get into the head" of the characters whom they portray (again, there's that assumption that it's all in the head), but the goal is simply to behave, on stage or screen, in a way that makes the audience accept the portrayed character as real. Novelists and other writers also work at trying to understand or describe what it is like to be someone else, especially when a novel includes a lot of the internal dialogue or thoughts and feelings of a character. Either way it's a hard task. For my whole life, I've only experienced what it is like to be Me, and that makes it very difficult to really imagine what it's like to be someone else.

Taking this thought a step further, it is even more difficult to imagine what it is like to be some*thing* else—that is, something other than a human being. When my son Ziv was 8 or 9, he was a great fan of a series of books called *Animorphs*. The stories, written by science fiction author K. A. Applegate, focus on the adventures of a group of youngsters who, as a result of an encounter with an alien, have the power to "acquire" the DNA of various animals and then become those animals for periods of time. They use this wonderful power to fight bad guys. The scope of such stories is limited only by the number of animals that the author might think of as her subjects. The remarkable thing about the books was that the author had her characters "morph" into animals—a tiger, a hawk, an ant, and so on—and then describe the experience through the sense of self of that animal. This is an incredible feat of authorial imagination. For as difficult as it is for me to imagine what it is like to be a different person, I cannot begin to imagine what it is like to be a dog, a dolphin, or a pigeon. The problem of such a feat of imagination was eloquently stated by philosopher Thomas Nagel in a fascinating article entitled "What Is It Like to Be a Bat?" He wrote:

> Our own experience provides the basic material for our imagination, whose range is therefore limited. It will not help to try to imagine that one has webbing on one's arms, which enables one to fly around at dusk and dawn catching insects in one's mouth; that one has very poor vision and perceives the surrounding world by a system of reflected high-frequency sound signals; and that one spends the day hanging upside down by one's feet in an attic. In so far as I can imagine this (which is not very far), it tells me only what it would be like for *me* to behave as a bat behaves. But that is not the question. I want to know what it is like for a *bat* to be a bat. Yet if I try to imagine this, I am restricted to the resources of my own mind, and those resources are inadequate to the task. I cannot perform it either by imagining additions to my present experience, or by imagining segments gradually subtracted from it, or by imagining some combination of additions, subtractions, and modifications.[13]

Nagel goes on to point out that the fact that we cannot possibly imagine what a bat's experience and consciousness are like for the bat should in no way lead us to conclude that bats have no subjective experience or consciousness.

CONSCIOUSNESS AND RELATIONSHIP

Despite the impossibility of really imagining what it is like to be something else, or even someone else, it is nevertheless absolutely crucial that I assume that being someone else is something akin to what it is like to be Me. Without such an assumption, relationship and communication would be impossible. These fundamental human activities, forming relationships and communicating, are critically dependent on our assuming that others have consciousness similar to our own. Why is this so? Imagine this: A friend has inadvertently said or done something that has hurt my feelings. After stewing about it for a while, I decide to confront my friend. I explain how and why her behavior made me feel hurt and what in my own background made me unusually sensitive to what should have been an unimportant comment or act. My explanation concludes with, "So you understand why I was so upset?" My friend thinks a moment and then gushes an apology for having hurt me. The whole exchange is predicated on the assumption on *both* our parts that what it is like to be Me (that is, my consciousness) is fairly similar to what it is like to be her (that is, her consciousness). Both of us must be able to imagine ourselves in the other's shoes—an interesting turn of a phrase, given the above discussion about the fact that consciousness takes place in our heads—or else my attempt to explain my distress would be meaningless, and her understanding and subsequent remorse would be impossible.

Now there are clearly different kinds of relationships and interactions, and not all require the same degree or depth of this assumption. So when I cuddle and sing to an infant, trying to calm and comfort him, the level of the assumption is not very high. All that is needed for the interaction to "work" is physical contact, gentle and soothing humming, and body language that telegraphs caring and nurture. The same behaviors work as well if I am trying to calm an excited puppy, though I clearly do not need to assume very much about the similarity of my consciousness and the puppy's. In general, we may say that the more sophisticated and complicated the content of the interaction or relationship, the more I must assume that my "other" is similar to me with regard to subjective experience.

What would happen, though, if I wanted or needed to enter into an interactive relationship with an other who was totally unlike me? This has been a conundrum to science fiction writers for as long as the genre has existed. Would the little green ambassador from Planet X be able to interact with us at all? The question has been widely skirted by having nearly all such fictional aliens be remarkably similar—even in their general body structure—to humans. Beyond the realm of fiction, the problem cannot be avoided. As scientists have planned for possible future attempts to communicate with extraterrestrial intelligent life, they have sometimes assumed that the "basic" language of mathematics would be the logical place to start. But even this assumption is predicated on a certain similarity between our human minds and the minds of extraterrestrials. It is indeed difficult to imagine how we would communicate with life forms radically different in structure from us.

What about God? If it is hard to imagine how we could communicate with extraterrestrials, it should be vastly more difficult to imagine how to communicate with God. For, as we have seen, the possibility of communication rests on certain explicit or implicit assumptions about the degree of similarity in the mental and experiential life of the one with whom I would like to communicate. To put the problem bluntly, if it is impossible for us to know—or even imagine—what it is like to be a bat, how much the more so to imagine what it is like to be God!

This problem seemed not to bother the ancients. The mythologies of a wide range of ancient civilizations portray their deities as bigger, stronger versions of human beings. They plan and brood, rejoice and get angry, aspire, achieve, and fail, much as we do. It would not have been substantially more difficult to communicate with such gods than to communicate with one's local chieftain or one's parent or older sibling. The disparity in power and strength between me and the one with whom I wish to communicate does not change the basic similarity in structure, substance, and experience between us.

To a great extent, the ancient Hebrews imagined their God in similarly human-like form. Thus we read in the Torah of God being pleased or satisfied with what He created (Gen. 1:31), regretting having made the deeply flawed humans (Gen. 6:6), worrying that humans are becoming too powerful (Gen. 11:6), making promises to Abram (Gen. 15), negotiating with Abraham (Gen. 18), hearing the outcry of the enslaved Israelites and remembering the covenant with them (Ex. 6:5), becoming enraged at the Israelites and then being mollified by Moses (Ex. 32:9–14), and so on. All these descriptions are completely human in nature. The overall impression that we get from the Hebrew Bible is that if kings have power, God is the King with the most power, and if gods have vast power, God's power is vaster than that of any of them. God is clearly at the very top of the continuous hierarchy that joins all creatures, but God *is a part of the continuum.*

In the postbiblical period that saw the development of Rabbinic Judaism, this situation did not change much. Even though the rabbis perceived God as being somewhat less involved in human affairs on a day-to-day level (there were, for example, no more prophets getting direct divine input), they still imagined God being rather person-like. There are rabbinic teachings that prescribe human behavior modeled on divine behavior—for example, we are to visit the sick just as God visited the sick; we are to put on *tefillin* (phylacteries) just as God does; we are to be gracious and merciful just as God is; and so on. The frequent insertion in rabbinic texts about God of the Hebrew word *kiv'yakhol,* meaning "as it were," is a sign that the rabbis were beginning to feel a bit uncomfortable with such an anthropomorphic God, but the word is more a hedge against anthropomorphism than a retreat from or rejection of it.

But with the rise of medieval rationalism, Jewish thinkers began to reject such anthropomorphism in a big way. The best known of them, and the most influential on later Jewish thought, was Maimonides (Rambam; Rabbi Moses Ben Maimon, 1135–1204). He leaves no doubt about his views on the matter in his "Thirteen Principles," a set of short statements of belief that appear first in Rambam's commentary to the Mishnah, but in modern times are often included at the end of the morning service in traditional prayer books.[14] The statements, each of which begins with the opening formula "I believe with a perfect faith [*Ani ma'amin b'emunah shlema*]," include these two:

> I believe with perfect faith that the Creator (may His name be blessed) is unique, and there is no uniqueness at all like Him, that He alone was, is, and will be our God.
> I believe with perfect faith that the Creator (may His name be blessed) is not corporeal [i.e., has no physical form] and is not affected by physical phenomena, and that nothing whatsoever exists that is in any way similar to Him.

These two statements raise some very serious questions regarding my earlier observations about the natural human assumption that an other with whom I interact must be more or less like me. In the normal course of our daily communications, we always assume—whether consciously or not—that other people's experiential repertoires are the same as our own. Maimonides clearly rejects the possibility that God is "like us" in *any way whatsoever*. God cannot have experiences that are in any way similar to, or even analogous to, ours.

The absolute nature of this position leaves me frankly at a loss to understand how to conceive of any real possibility of communicating or being in a relationship with God. And so, although Maimonides's assertions made their way into the daily prayer book at some point and became the basis for the rather vague and imprecise theological truths that we are taught as little children (truths such as "of course you can't *see* God!"), I think that most of us have never considered the implications of such teachings. Because our thought is so powerfully conditioned by our language (we actually think in words), we have little choice but to imagine that the traditional language that we use to describe God actually has some representational meaning. When the Torah tells us that God got angry, it is absolutely natural and unavoidable for us to understand that statement as meaning roughly what the statement "I got angry" means. That is the way language works. Words have meaning and the whole system of language is based on the fact that the meaning of a word stays more or less constant as it is applied to a variety of things. Thus "My friend got angry," and "The stormy sea looked angry," and "The burn I received when I touched the frying pan yesterday turned an angry shade of red," all have at least a vaguely similar sense. If Maimonides tells us that

"God got angry" has *nothing at all* to do with any other uses of the word, then words become meaningless.

Here is the central point: We are engaged in an investigation of God's consciousness. If we imagine that God *does have* consciousness but we also assume, following Maimonides, that God's consciousness bears absolutely no resemblance to our consciousness, then our entire investigation will be utterly futile. The main reason for the quest that is at the heart of this book is my sense that a full and deep Judaism *requires* that God interact with us humans. The notion of a *covenant* between God and the Jewish people, first introduced in the stories of Abraham in Genesis and developed throughout all subsequent generations of Jewish thinkers, is critically dependent on communication and interaction with God. In order to find a God who can interact with us, I must reject all claims of God's absolute uniqueness. The first chapter of Genesis lays down a basic element of what it means to be human: We are created "in God's image." Minimally, this assertion requires that there be some similarity between God and us.

THE PLAN

In the following pages, I will try to create a clear, rational model by which we might think of God as being conscious and thus being able to interact with us. I will first sketch out some of the basic notions from contemporary cognitive science about how human consciousness works. I will then propose a way to apply a current model of human consciousness to the realm of God, focusing especially on the idea of *emergence*. I will point out the way in which the model makes Judaism more plausible, more compelling, for me. Finally, I will examine the questions and concerns that the model may raise.

When I teach, my goal is never to "browbeat" skeptical students into agreeing with my position by wielding either my authority over them or my academic credentials. Instead my goal is to present ideas, often in the form of questions, that will encourage my students to think, challenge, and come to their own conclusions. Sometimes they accept the ideas I have proposed and sometimes they reject them, preferring their own approaches. I measure my success not by the degree to which my students agree with me, but by the depth, creativity, and thoughtfulness of the conversation. My goal in what lies ahead here is the same. I hope that some readers will agree, although I know that others—perhaps many—will not. But I will measure my success by the extent to which the ideas I shall present here stimulate thought and conversation.

NOTES

1. See the beginning of *Yotzer*, the first of the two blessings preceding the *Sh'ma* in the daily morning prayer service.
2. Harold Morowitz, *The Emergence of Everything* (New York: Oxford University Press, 2002), 21–22.
3. It is customary to refer to them as "*laws* of nature," but this can be misleading. We usually use the word "law" to describe a rule enacted by a human being or organization to regulate the behavior of human beings. But such laws can be broken, though doing so may result in punishment. By contrast, "laws" of nature cannot be broken. They describe how the universe works, to the best of our knowledge. If one succeeds in breaking a law of nature, the conclusion must be that what was thought to have been a law was in fact not an accurate description of nature, and thus that law must be discarded and replaced by a better one—that is, one that more accurately describes the universe.
4. The American Heritage Dictionary of the English Language, Fourth Edition .
5. I began these observations speaking about "Western revealed religion" in general, but since both this book and my expertise are in Judaism in particular, I will hereafter restrict my analysis to Jewish thought and belief.
6. Two pages later Hawkins specifies the date of this first interest: September 1979.
7. Jeff Hawkins and Sandra Blakeslee, *On Intelligence* (New York: Henry Holt and Co., 2004), 7–8.
8. Jer. 4:19.
9. The first phrase is a quotation from Prov. 20:27; the second is from Jer. 11:20.
10. Morris Silverman (ed.), *High Holiday Prayer Book* (Hartford, CT: Prayer Book Press, 1956), 270 and elsewhere.
11. Nosson Scherman (trans.), *The Complete ArtScroll Machzor: Yom Kippur* (Brooklyn, NY: Mesorah Publications, 1986), 359 and elsewhere.
12. It is important, even if somewhat obvious, to note that this sense of self is normally experienced as being contained within a body. For the human experience, this feature of consciousness only becomes noteworthy when we hear of someone reporting an out-of-body experience—a rare and perplexing event—or, more often, when someone we know dies and we are confronted by all sorts of aching questions about where the "self" of the person is. Has it ceased to exist? Does it continue to exist as a disembodied soul? These are overwhelmingly difficult questions that I will not attempt to address here.
13. Thomas Nagel, "What Is It Like to Be a Bat?" *Philosophical Review* (October 1974), Vol. LXXXIII, 435–450.
14. See, for example, Philip Birnbaum, *Daily Prayer Book* (New York: Hebrew Publishing Company, 1969), 174ff.; Nosson Scherman et al., *The Complete ArtScroll Siddur* (New York: Mesorah Publications, 1984), 179ff.; and many other popular prayer books.

Chapter Two

The Brain, The Mind, and Consciousness

BASIC DISTINCTIONS

When I was a little boy, a favorite family game was Twenty Questions, where one player thought of a thing and the others tried to guess what the thing was by asking no more than twenty questions, each of which had to be answerable with a simple yes or no. But the game started with a hint. The one who had picked the secret thing had to tell the others whether the thing in question was animal, vegetable, or mineral. This initial statement of broad category narrowed the task considerably. What did it tell us? Minimally, if the thing was "mineral," then we would expect it to not move around, not eat, sleep, reproduce, or perform other biological functions, and to be more or less inert. Rock-like. "Vegetable," on the other hand, would tell us that the item in question probably started as a seed of some sort, grew larger, needed some sort of nutrients (air, water, food through its roots), and had some sort of mechanism for reproducing itself—flowers, seed pods, etc. But it also told us that it probably didn't have a brain that would allow it to plan or to move volitionally to a better location (e.g., out of danger or to a place with a richer food supply), though it might well have a means of scattering its offspring with the help of wind, insects, animals, and so on. "Animal," of course, placed on the list of possibilities all those things that do plan, look out for their own welfare, and respond volitionally to their environment. This childhood game concealed many deep and fascinating assumptions about the basic distinctions that we see in the world.[1]

In the 1970s there was a bit of a fad over growing houseplants. Urban sophisticates grew all sorts of exotic things in pots and spent a good deal of effort researching how to do it better. For a while there was a notion that talking to your plants made them grow better. I never put much stock in this theory. After all, the initial step of my childhood Twenty Questions games taught me to distinguish between vegetables and animals. A large part of this distinction seemed to have been based on the animal's ability to experience the environment—that is, to be aware of it, to interact with it—while vegetables just sit there in their pots or their gardens or forests and grow. My intuition does not permit me to see plants as having the ability to be aware of their environment or have feelings, the way animals do. In fact, even when plants do respond to their environment (as when a plant turns toward a light source), I assume that this is a strictly biomechanical action—that is, it is one of the properties built into the plant by means of evolution—rather than being the result of a "choice" made by the plant, the way I might choose to walk around a puddle instead of getting my shoes wet.

In fact, volitional choice, thought, experience, and feeling are characteristic features that I generally assume to be limited to the animal kingdom. Within the animal kingdom, distinctions become a bit trickier. That is to say, there is not a shred of doubt in my mind that my dogs have thoughts and feelings. They are clearly *excited* and *happy* when I arrive home after a long day away. They *enjoy* riding in the car. One of them *dislikes* going for walks in the rain: when I open the door and she sees that it is raining hard, she locks her knees and refuses to budge. They exhibit clear signs of emotion on a level so noticeable that I am certain that what I am seeing is not simply my human emotions projected onto them. The situation is less clear when I think of far simpler (that is, "lower"; we value consciousness so much that we establish hierarchies related to its presence or absence) creatures—fish, insects, or single-celled microscopic organisms. These creatures are clearly alive. They react to the environment, avoiding danger, seeking food, and moving purposefully. I imagine, however, that they have less of an experiential world. This assumption comes from the simplicity of their brains and nervous systems. The consensus, based on the modern understanding of life, is that experience, thought, feeling, and consciousness are functions of brains, and that the larger and more complex the brain, the richer and more complex the experiential landscape, the consciousness, of the creature. Cognitive scientist Douglas Hofstadter has somewhat whimsically described a hierarchy of "different sized souls," ranging from those with "lots of consciousness" (normal adult humans), through those with some, but less, consciousness (dogs, rabbits, chickens, goldfish) to the "smallest" souls that have little or no consciousness (microbes, viruses, atoms). He is careful to point out that by "soul" he does not mean some religiously imagined, immaterial spirit, but rather the awareness, consciousness, or sense of self with which we are familiar.[2]

PRIMARY CONSCIOUSNESS IN THE UNIVERSE

Some cognitive scientists refer to the minimal sort of consciousness that entails being somewhat aware of one's inner state, and being sufficiently aware of one's external environment to respond to it purposefully, as primary consciousness. They use the term "higher-order consciousness" to describe the reflective, contemplative, self-aware state that is so characteristic of human beings and allows us to ask, "What does it mean to be conscious?"[3] This distinction in terminology is useful, since it gives us a way to distinguish the kind of consciousness that dogs and cows and birds clearly have from the kind that humans have—but which we cannot say with certainty that other creatures have.[4]

Primary consciousness is a pretty remarkable thing. We only notice just how remarkable it is when we think of the multitude of objects in the universe that do not possess it as one of their characteristics. Consider a star. It comes into existence as the result of complex processes involving the accretion of hydrogen atoms into a cloud. The cloud becomes larger and denser as the force of gravity compresses it. This compression raises the temperature until finally the atoms that comprise it begin to fuse, causing a chain reaction, the release of enormous amounts of energy, and the birth of a star. The star then goes through a sequence of stages, its life cycle, during which its properties—its size, and the amount and types of energy it radiates—change, until finally it dies and its form changes in any of several, highly predictable ways.

Note that in the last two sentences I used the words "birth," "life cycle," and "dies." All these words come from the realm of biology and are properly used to describe living organisms, but their use in connection with a star is strictly metaphorical. Stars are not alive. They do not die. The natural laws that govern their existence and give them their characteristics are truly awesome. Without stars we humans would not exist. Throughout the history of the universe, stars function as the "chemical factories" in which the elements that make up our planet and our bodies are manufactured. And the radiation given off by our neighborhood star (the sun) is absolutely essential for the initial origin of life on earth and our continued ability to live. Without it there would be no liquid water, no oxygen, no food. It is the source of all life on earth. As such, it is completely appropriate that human beings have always had a tremendous reverence for the sun. Ancient civilizations worshipped it as a god. In Jewish tradition the authors of our most ancient teachings cautioned us not to worship the sun, but only the one God who created it. Yet the sun still plays an important part in our liturgy. Every morning our liturgy praises God as the one who "fashions light and creates darkness," and every evening it credits God with "ordering the stars in their courses in the sky." The sun is a wondrous thing. Yet for all this, it is *not* alive. It does not sense its environment and cannot control its destiny. Its behavior, motion, and characteristics are completely governed by the laws of physics.

Now compare the sun with a small fish. As awe inspiring as the sun is, the fish is even more so. Aside from the many incredible features that come from its simply being alive (e.g., the fact that it can reproduce), it has primary consciousness. It can sense its internal and external environment and respond to them. So, for example, when the fish needs food (that is, feels hunger), it moves from a location in which there is no food to another in which there is food. And when it senses danger in its environment—a predator, for example—it escapes or hides or behaves in some other manner to avoid being eaten. Even if we are careful not to project human experiences onto the fish but interpret this behavior as being completely driven by instinct, it is still quite impressive. A star cannot sense its internal or external environment or do anything to affect its position. If it is about to be struck by another star, it is not aware of the impending disaster, nor can it avoid it. The fish can.

What accounts for this fundamental difference between stars, ocean waves, tectonic plates, and rain clouds on the one hand, and even very simple forms of life on the other? The answer is brains or, somewhat more precisely, nervous systems. These are networks of nerve cells called neurons that use a combination of electrical and chemical means to transmit information from one part of a complex organism to another. A neuron is composed of three main parts. The cell body, or soma, is the central core of the cell, including its nucleus. Each neuron also contains a set of dendrites, known collectively as the dendritic tree (so called because of its form, many branches coming off the soma), which function as the input mechanism of the neuron—that is, the places where information is received by the neuron. Finally, the neuron has an axon, a sort of extension cable that extends from the soma and carries information from the neuron to other neurons, thus constituting the output portion of the neuron. The juncture at which the axon of one neuron meets a dendrite of another (that is, the place where the transmission of signal between one neuron and another actually occurs) is called the synapse.

When a neuron is stimulated, by receiving via its dendrites an electrical impulse—or action potential—from another neuron or another anatomical organ (e.g., a signal that light has fallen on the retina of the eye or that sound has caused a vibration in the structures of the ear), it transmits the impulse via its axon to other neurons or anatomical structures.[5] Through the functioning of this system, the following simple process can occur: A lizard sitting on a rock is approached by a bird that eats lizards. The lizard's eyes register the bird's approach; the patterns of bird-shaped form, color, and movement are picked up by the lizard's eyes. This visual information is transmitted by neurons from the lizard's eyes to its brain, where the information is processed in such a way that results in other neuronal signals being generated to the lizard's muscles, causing it to scamper under the rock to avoid being eaten. I have been careful to avoid personifying the lizard by saying, for example, that it *understands* the danger in the bird's approach, is *frightened* by the prospect of being eaten, or *decides* to hide under the rock. It is quite possible that the lizard experiences nothing that is similar to our human experience of *understanding,* being *frightened,* or *deciding,* but that the entire process takes place on the level of reflexes and instincts—meaning on an automatic level requiring no understanding, thought, or conscious decision making. Perhaps what happens in the lizard is similar to the level of response that I experience when something comes toward my face—say, a low-hanging tree branch over a sidewalk on which I am strolling without paying much attention. As the branch approaches my eyes, I close my eyes and move my head before I even become consciously aware that there is a branch there. My eyes and brain have a built-in "collision avoidance system" that functions whether or not I am paying attention. The difference between me and the lizard, I imagine (though remember that we cannot know what it is like to be a bat or a lizard), is that after avoiding the branch I may marvel at the outstanding neuroanatomical engineering with which I have been blessed, or I may "thank my lucky stars" at the close call that could easily have resulted in an eye injury. If I am a traditionally religious person, I might even recite a brief prayer of thanks to God for saving me from danger. All these, I imagine, are behaviors not available to the lizard. They are what distinguish the lizard's primary consciousness from my higher-order consciousness.

Primary consciousness exists in animals with relatively simple, small, and primitive[6] brains. Higher-order consciousness, on the other hand, is what distinguishes us as human beings from most other animals. It includes the ability to have a sense of Me (that is, of self) and the ability to reflect, think, imagine, make moral judgments, and reason in semantic and linguistic terms. It is largely what makes us human. Higher-order consciousness *presupposes* the presence of primary consciousness; one cannot have higher-order consciousness without primary consciousness, but it is possible to have primary consciousness without higher-order consciousness.

HIGHER-ORDER CONSCIOUSNESS

Higher-order consciousness is a function of the most recently evolved part of the brain, the neocortex. The neocortex is a six-layered sheet of nerve tissue, about two millimeters (almost a tenth of an inch) thick, that covers the topmost part of the brain. If it were uncrinkled and spread flat, it would be about the size of a large dinner napkin. In proportion to our body size, this makes it the largest neocortex by far of any other animal, and it is the sheer size of the neocortex that makes us so "smart." There is no generally accepted estimate of the number of neurons in the neocortex, but one estimate puts the number at about 30 billion.[7] The most important feature of the neocortex seems to be the massive interconnectedness of its neurons. That is, the neurons are linked to one another in hugely complex networks that connect and reconnect with one another to produce a staggering number and array of linkages. One neuroscientist, describing how any given region of the neocortex receives input patterns from thousands or millions of axons, suggests that "[t]he number of possible patterns that can exist on even one thousand axons is larger than the number of molecules in the universe."[8]

Most neuroscientists seem to agree that this interconnectedness is largely responsible for the functioning of the neocortex in producing what we experience as consciousness. Neural signals travel back and forth in feedback loops between and among vast numbers of cortical areas in all layers of the neocortex, so that each neuron is constantly in communication with many, many other neurons and, via countless recursive feedback loops, in communication with itself. This complex interconnectedness seems to be at the heart of the process.

There is also widespread agreement on the idea that consciousness is not created or mediated by one specific localized region, or organ, of the brain. This is a tremendously important insight. When the seventeenth century philosopher René Descartes (1596–1650) studied the mind, he theorized that the seat of consciousness (the soul) was located in the pineal gland, a small endocrine gland located deep in the center of the brain. This theory led to a search for the particular part of the brain responsible for consciousness. But now, even though a great deal of work is being done to map the locations of brain function dealing, for example, with vision, hearing, motor activity, and many other specific activities, the consensus is that consciousness itself does not reside in any one localized brain area. Rather, it is a widely distributed function.

THE ORIGIN OF CONSCIOUSNESS

Let's briefly review the history of consciousness, for although we cannot imagine existence without it, consciousness has not always been a feature of our universe.[9] Cosmologists put the origin of the universe in the Big Bang somewhere between 13 and 14 billion years ago. The Milky Way Galaxy, in which our solar system is located, came into being about 10 billion years ago. Our solar system was formed about 4.7 billion years ago, with planet Earth just a bit later than that. According to the oldest known fossils, bacteria and blue-green algae appeared by about 3.5 billion years ago, and by about 2 billion years ago plants capable of photosynthesis had appeared. Photosynthesis in plants resulted in the beginnings of a significant oxygen atmosphere here on Earth about 1.3 billion years ago. The first worms appeared 625 million years ago, with fish and vertebrates (animals with backbones) appearing about 500 million years ago. (Note that according to biologist Harold Morowitz, the first neurons may well have evolved in a group of organisms called *cnidarians*, which includes coral, jellyfish, sea anemones, and more, as much as 700 million years ago.[10] This detail will become very important as we progress.) The first insects appeared 400 million years ago and the first dinosaurs about 250 million years ago. By 200 million years ago the first mammals began to appear, but it took until about 50 million years ago for all the mammalian orders to appear. It was only between about 20 million and 10 million years ago that the so-called great apes—orangutans, baboons, gorillas, and chimpanzees—appeared. The first evidence known so far of the branch of the evolutionary tree on which we humans eventually grew is only about 6 million years old,[11] and while there is still disagreement as to exactly when modern humans (that is, *Homo sapiens*) first appeared, paleontologists agree that this event occurred less than 200,000 years ago.

What we see from this very rough sketch, even if we take all the dates as being only approximations, is that based on the evidence available to us, the vast bulk of the history of the universe up to this point did not include anything with a nervous system or a brain, and therefore—at least according to the intuition I described earlier in this chapter—did not include anything with mind, awareness, or consciousness. Even if we think only about primary consciousness, and imagine that the first worms possessed such rudimentary awareness of their internal and external environments, we find that these abilities characterize only about the last 4–5 percent of the total history of the cosmos. And if we focus exclusively on higher-order consciousness, and imagine it to have appeared with the very first great apes, then we see that this true awareness characterizes only the most recent 0.14 percent of the history of the universe. To put it another way, for most of its history the universe—at least our corner of it[12]—has been devoid of thought, awareness, mind, and consciousness. In the animal/vegetable/mineral taxonomy of my childhood, most of the life of the cosmos to date has been "mineral."

PRIMARY VERSUS HIGHER-ORDER CONSCIOUSNESS

Equipped with this rudimentary sense of the history of the evolution of life, nervous systems, brains, and minds, let's return briefly to the distinction between different kinds of processes that occur in different brains. We saw in the above description of the lizard escaping a predatory bird by moving under a rock, a wonderful example of a highly sophisticated set of brain processes. The lizard's eyes can detect the visual cues associated with the movement of things nearby (this all by itself is remarkable), but the lizard is able to detect and categorize enough details of the things moving in its vicinity to make some very important distinctions. It can distinguish, for example, between a leaf that is blown by a gust of wind, an insect that not only presents no threat but presents an opportunity for a potential meal, and that predatory bird moving in for the kill. Based on those fine distinctions, it can decide which action to take, ranging from no action in the case of the leaf, to the sequence of actions needed to hunt for and eat food in the case of the insect, to the complicated set of behaviors needed to evade the predator in the case of the bird. The evasion itself requires a highly coordinated set of perceptual and musculoskeletal tasks—judging from what direction the threat is coming, seeking out a satisfactory place of refuge, and moving its body quickly to that place. This is a complex and sophisticated process. It takes place in the lizard in a split second. With our current engineering and technological capabilities, we could not possibly build a mechanical device that could react so effectively, so fast, or so reliably. The lizard's abilities to perform these tasks are the crux of primary consciousness. Yet it *may* very well be that the lizard has no awareness of the event, in a higher-order sense. Why is this significant? Compare the lizard's experience with a parallel human experience. I am walking along the streets on a rainy day and I am vaguely aware of a large puddle in the street nearby. I suddenly notice a truck zooming along in the lane closest to me. I jump back just far enough to avoid getting soaked as the truck splashes through the grimy water. Unfortunately, although I escape unscathed, other pedestrians who are less agile or attentive are soaked.

So far little distinguishes my experience from the lizard's. I have visually processed elements of my environment, made a determination that they pose a threat to me, and avoided that threat by my behavior. These actions are the essence of primary consciousness. But then my experience continues to develop in a way that we do not believe the lizard's can. I *think* to myself that I was very lucky to jump back far enough. I *imagine* how uncomfortable I would have been if I had had to spend the day in pants soaked and stained. I *communicate* via glances, sympathetic nods, and a few words with my fellow pedestrians ("What awful weather" or "Drivers are such jerks!"). Throughout the day I *tell stories* about my brush with disaster. In short, I reflect on my experience and communicate with others about it. I evaluate it and see patterns in it (even when they may not really exist, as I may complain, "It always seems to rain on days when I have to get dressed up for something important!"). These actions are characteristic of higher-order consciousness. They involve the ability to create a mental narrative in which there is a character called "Me" and to think about that narrative, talk about it, and wonder about it.

This scenario is an ordinary part of the way that we humans function. Yet, according to neuroscientists, it is a huge mystery. Researchers still have no detailed understanding of how, not to mention why, these elements of higher-order consciousness function. Those with an evolutionary bent are certain that they confer some survival advantage on us, and at some level it is not hard to see why. When we go beyond the simple avoidance of danger to telling stories about it, these stories can educate our young, thereby teaching them to behave in a more prudent fashion. In this way each generation need not discover the dangers of rainy days or hungry predators or deadly diseases on its own, but can learn about these threats from prior generations. This is a process sometimes referred to as cultural evolution (as opposed to biological evolution). The group that teaches its children most effectively flourishes best. It is much less clear why we as a species go on to dream about our experiences, write and read fictional accounts of experiences that did not really happen, develop religious beliefs based on experience, and so on. Nor is it at all clear *how* these things happen in the brain.

What does seem fairly clear is that these fantastic abilities cannot be traced to a single area of the brain. If we look at a whole brain, in a whole person, and begin to break down its functioning into its component parts, we find only one basic thing: neurons, connected to a vast number of other neurons, each firing electrochemical signals across synapses when it is stimulated in turn by the neurons that are signaling it. That's all that happens in the brain. Nowhere do we find the calculating-how-far-back-to-jump-to-avoid-getting-splashed brain area or the telling-my-wife-about-the-rainy-commute brain area. They simply don't exist. Yet when we put tens of billions of neurons together in a brain, dress it up, and send it out on a rainy day, these are exactly the processes that occur. So if they're not happening in any particular neuron or region of neurons, where are they happening? What's going on?

DUALISM VERSUS PHYSICALISM

The question of how electrochemical signaling across synapses by neurons could produce what we experience as consciousness is a perplexing one that has mystified thinkers and researchers at least since the time of René Descartes. Descartes spent a great deal of time thinking about mind and consciousness, and in fact is probably best known for his formulation *cogito ergo sum* ("I think, therefore I am"). Among his conclusions was the notion that the human body is basically a machine that functions in ways similar to all machines and obeys the laws of physics, mechanics, and so on. The body is composed of *res extens* or "extended thing" (in other words, physical stuff that behaves in fairly well understood ways). On the other hand, Descartes asserted, the human mind (or soul) is of a different category. It is *not* machine-like and is *not* physical. According to Descartes, it is a fundamentally different sort of stuff, which he called *res cogitans* or "mental thing." As such, it does not follow physical laws and cannot be understood as a mechanism in a world of mechanisms.

This notion that body and mind are made of fundamentally different categories of stuff is called dualism, since it divides the world into two basic categories. In many ways it makes sense intuitively. We can easily imagine the process of vision, for example, as a mechanical, physical process, analogous to that which happens in a machine like a camera. When light falls on the retina, it stimulates a signal that is transmitted via the optic nerve to another part of the brain where the signal is processed. This sounds very much like what happens when light enters the lens of a video camera and stimulates an electrical signal that is carried in a cable to a mechanism that processes the signal and results in an image appearing on a television screen. But it doesn't take much contemplation to realize that this is not all there is to our experience of seeing. In fact, the description of the video camera, cable, and television screen is missing one critical element—namely, the presence of a person watching the screen. From a subjective point of view, we understand the idea that when we look at a red flower the image enters the eye, gets turned upside down by the lens of the eye, falls on the retina at the back of the eye, and sends signals via the optic nerve to the visual cortex at the back of the brain; but then it seems that we need the critical (and mysterious) step of imagining someone, some little conscious self, watching the "screen" in the visual cortex. Philosopher Daniel Dennett refers to this subjective intuition as the Cartesian Theater.[13] The mind, according to this dualist notion, is the little audience that watches what happens on the screen of the theater. We come to this conclusion because we know that a video camera does not "see" red flowers; it simply records and transmits images. Seeing is more than what happens in a camera. It is what happens when people stand in an art museum drinking in the hues and being mesmerized by the subtle power of a painting. That is a conscious behavior, a mind behavior. It does seem, in accordance with Descartes's understanding, to be different from the mechanical process of signal transmission. And it is very hard, perhaps even impossible, to imagine how simple electrochemical signals running through the "wiring" in our brains could produce the experience of awe that we get gazing at the sun setting over a lake. But the problem is that neuroanatomists over the centuries, even today in an age of MRIs and ever-increasing knowledge of the brain's structure, have never found any little theater in there, with a tiny screen, little plush seats, and a miniscule person sitting there watching it all. Neurons and synapses seem to be all that's under the hood. That difficulty leads some thinkers, following in Descartes's footsteps, to believe that the process of seeing and being awed—that is, the process of consciousness—*must* be made of, and driven by, fundamentally different stuff from that which drives the mechanism of image processing.

In contrast to dualism,[14] there is a school of thought known as monism. Monists reject the notion that there are two fundamental types of stuff in the universe and insist that all things, all phenomena, are made of the same stuff—that is, that there is only one fundamental type of stuff in the universe, not two. A prominent type of monism is physicalism, which insists that all of reality can and must be explained in terms of physics—that is, in terms of the physical stuff, the matter and energy, that constitutes the universe and the laws that regulate the behavior of that stuff. This is the school of thought often associated with hard-boiled rationalists who find dualism much too spooky for their tastes. After all, if we can't see it or detect it, it's probably not there. To assume that it is there, despite all the hard evidence that it isn't, is unscientific. And while such folks are not closed to the possibility that there might be some kind of matter or energy that we haven't yet discovered—after all, in the 1950s we thought that protons, neutrons, and electrons were as "fundamental" as fundamental particles could get, until quarks, muons, gluons, bosons, and the rest came along—they reject the possibility that there are fundamental pieces of reality that are not essentially susceptible to comprehension by the laws of physics.

THE LOGIC OF REDUCTIONISM

Closely associated with physicalism is a scientific approach known as reductionism. Reductionism is the view that any complex object or phenomenon can be understood by breaking it down (that is, "reducing" it—hence the name) into its component parts, then breaking them down into their component parts, and so on until you reach the simplest level. In other words, the underlying composition of a complicated thing holds the secrets to its essence. A classic example is the proposition that all biology is understandable as chemistry, and that all chemistry is understandable as physics. What does this mean? Biology is the study of living things. But living things are so complex, and so mysterious. The complexity seems to fall away, though, and much of the mystery along with it, when we understand biological processes in terms of the chemistry that underlies them. So a cell—say, a muscle cell that, when acting together with lots of other muscle cells, allows me to hold a ping pong paddle—is best understood by seeing the chemistry that explains its structure and function. The cell is made up of certain chemicals, and their properties allow certain types of chemicals to pass into the cell, while keeping other chemicals out. The process of muscle contraction, necessary to grasp and lift the ping pong paddle, is regulated by various chemical interactions in and around the cell.

By understanding chemistry, we can simplify and thereby understand such complex and wondrous phenomena as the fact that my muscles require oxygen and fuel. If deprived of either or both, they get tired. When this happens, if I breathe deeply and have a snack, I feel more energetic. It's not magic or mystery, just chemistry. But, the reductionists continue, even the marvels of chemistry are not so mysterious when we understand them as the product of the underlying physics. The reason the cell lets some chemicals in and keeps others out has to do with the compounds that are the building blocks of the cell, how they interact with each other, and how the atomic structure influences the constitution of these compounds. The behavior of the atoms as they interact with one another is governed by the laws of physics.

Reductionism functions as a core element of the scientific method by seeking understanding through analysis. Indeed, the etymology of the word "analysis" tells us something important: *ana* means "throughout" in Greek and *lysis* comes from the Greek *luein*, meaning "to loosen."[15] So *analysis* is the loosening of all the connections that hold together the pieces of a whole. The whole can be understood best by breaking it apart into its smallest component parts. This is the heart of reductionism.

There are many situations, however, in which reductionism proves to be an inadequate method for understanding an object or a system. A few examples will give us a sense of the problem. Consider first an iron wheel: Reductionism would urge that we take the wheel apart, breaking it down to its smallest components—that is to say, the iron atoms that make up the wheel's substance. If we were to do that, we would learn some things about the object. We would learn that it is metallic, that it has certain magnetic properties, that it conducts heat and electricity well, and so on. But this reductionist analysis would completely miss one of the most important properties of the original object—namely, that it rolls. In fact, rolling is a property of an iron wheel that is *only* present when the wheel is in its original form. As soon as anything is done to break it down (to "analyze" it), the property of rolling disappears.

Another example of the inadequacy of reductionism may be seen in the behavior of a crowd of people—say, the tens of thousands who may attend a major sporting event or a massive political rally. Reductionism would suggest that knowing how individuals behave would be sufficient to determine, understand, and predict the behavior of a crowd, since a crowd is (after all) just a gathering of a large number of individuals. Yet psychologists, police officials, and our common sense based on experience tell us that at a certain point the crowd begins to behave in ways that are unique to a crowd and cannot be understood as the sum of individual behaviors.

These examples, and countless others that we could look at, have often led back to a sort of dualism—that is, to an idea that if understanding the parts is not sufficient to gain an understanding of the whole, there must be more to the whole than just the parts that we see. The additional element must be something nonphysical, something mysterious, perhaps something spiritual. This is the core of dualism. But over the last few decades, another alternative has been suggested to this dualism. It is called emergence.[16]

DEFINING EMERGENCE

Emergence is the abstract label given to a phenomenon (which is then called an emergent phenomenon) that exhibits several key characteristics:

- In an emergent phenomenon, the whole is more than the sum of the parts, such that the workings of the whole cannot be understood solely by examining and understanding the working of the parts.
- The emergent phenomenon is on a new, higher level[17] than its parts; it is governed by rules that do not govern the parts, rules that are unique to its new level.
- The emergent phenomenon possesses properties or features that are not possessed by any of its constituent parts.
- The emergent phenomenon can and does exert downward causation on its constituent parts; that is, it can affect and influence them.

Each of these characteristics deserves some further explanation, but that explanation will make more sense if it is set in a context of some examples of emergent phenomena. Harold Morowitz has sketched out a chain of 28 emergences starting with the Big Bang and ending with the emergence of philosophy, spirituality, and religion.[18] It will help if we borrow an example from his chain, and then look at another from a completely ordinary part of our world.

The third step in Morowitz's 28-step chain is the emergence of stars in the early universe. Prior to this emergence, there were simply uneven patches in the widely distributed clouds of hydrogen and helium atoms, such that parts of the universe had denser concentrations of these simple particles while other parts had sparser concentrations of them. Gravitational forces made the denser patches more and more dense, drawing more and more particles into a smaller and smaller region. The increasing density led to increased levels of energy: the dense patches became hotter and hotter as their atoms, restricted by gravity to a smaller and smaller space, moved more quickly. As the temperature rose, a "proto-star" began to glow. As the hydrogen and helium atoms continued to accelerate, they reached a high enough energy level that their nuclei began to smash into each other with enough force to initiate fusion reactions (this is what happens in a hydrogen bomb). These reactions released vast amounts of energy and also synthesized other, heavier elements. An emergent phenomenon appeared; a star was born.

We can use this example to explain the four basic characteristics of any emergent phenomenon as laid out above. The star is clearly more than just the sum of its parts—namely, the hydrogen and helium atoms that constituted it. One can understand the behavior of these simple gases completely without having any insight into the workings of a star. The star is a new, higher-order phenomenon. The star's development and behavior are clearly defined by rules that are radically different from the rules governing clouds of hydrogen, helium, or individual atoms of either element. These are new rules of fusion and the synthesis of new, heavier elements that can only come into existence once the cloud has become sufficiently large, dense, and hot to begin the fusion reaction. The star also possesses properties and characteristics not possessed by clouds of hydrogen or helium. It glows with a fierce heat and it creates heavier elements. And finally, the star, as a new object, exerts a causative influence on its parts: the hydrogen and helium that make up such a first-generation[19] star end up being fused, converted into the nuclei of heavier elements, and "used up" (essentially, destroyed).

Our second example is found in a most modest and common substance—that is, ordinary water. It is made up of molecules, each of which consists of two hydrogen atoms bonded to an oxygen atom. These molecules behave in well-understood and highly predictable ways. But when a very large number of them are put together and energy is added to the mix so that the water molecules bump into each other (that is, they interact) in many ways, a strange bunch of characteristics appears. First of all, the water becomes wet. A single water molecule is not wet. The wetness comes only when we put a large number of molecules together. Second, the water flows. Single water molecules, or even very small numbers of them, don't do that. But perhaps the strangest characteristic that appears when a huge number of water molecules are put together and energy is added into the mix is turbulence, a phenomenon studied in great detail by the branch of physics known as chaos theory.

Turbulence is an emergent phenomenon that appears when energy is added to a flowing fluid. The flow transitions from what is called a laminar state—that is, a smooth state—to a turbulent one. The transition is caused by arbitrarily tiny perturbations (wrinkles, if you will) in the flow that interact with one another and with the water molecules in such highly complex ways that they are very difficult to understand, and virtually impossible to predict based on even the most detailed and thorough understanding of both the behavior of the water molecules and the smooth, gentle laminar flow prior to the onset of turbulence. Turbulence is itself a new phenomenon in the development of the stream of water. Not only can it not be predicted from—or understood through—a thorough understanding of the behavior of the particles that preceded its appearance, but it clearly has a causative effect on those particles; that is to say, it moves them around in ways that they could not and would not have moved without the onset of the turbulence. Like all emergent phenomena, it is a new and higher level in the development of the system.

By this point the concept of emergence (which is far easier to demonstrate by laying out examples than to define concisely) should be somewhat clearer, and you should begin to identify other commonplace instances of it. The behavior of a crowd or a mob is an emergent behavior, composed exclusively of the behaviors of the individual members of the group but neither predictable nor comprehensible based solely on an understanding of individual behavior. Likewise, the sweeping trends of a market are caused by nothing more than the sum total of the behaviors of a large number of buyers and sellers interacting with one another by buying and selling and by communicating in other ways about their buying and their selling. Yet understanding the behavior of the individual buyer or seller clearly is of little help in predicting how the market will behave. In this instance, even after-the-fact market news analysts are unsure of what accounted for today's major rise or fall in the market. Both of these examples also exhibit the important feature of downward causation: once the mob begins to get ugly, its behavior affects that of its individual members; and once a market hike or sell-off gathers steam, it carries the individual buyer or seller along in ways that they would not have been carried without the "big trend."

One more example of an emergent phenomenon comes from a relatively new, yet tremendously powerful and ubiquitous thing called the Internet. The Internet is nothing more than the sum total of billions of computers around the world linked to one another with some rather sophisticated communications protocols. The whole thing is so simple as to be easily understood by any 10-year-old getting homework help from an Internet search engine. Yet the Internet is *not* like the vast number of computers that underlie it. It operates by different rules and its behavior is not at all predictable if all you start with is knowledge of a personal computer. And it certainly can have profound impact on the individual computers that comprise it. It is clearly an emergent phenomenon.

All of these examples share two crucial features. First of all, they all involve a large number of individual parts. Four investors do not bring about major swings in the market, nor do two people on the street create a crowd. The number of hydrogen atoms necessary to give birth to a star, or of water molecules needed to create a turbulent flow, is simply too vast for most of us to comprehend. And hooking five or ten computers together does not create the Internet. And second, they all result from the intricate and complex *interaction* among all the large number of parts that underlie them. Large numbers and complex interactions appear to be at the heart of emergent phenomena.

EMERGENCE AND CONSCIOUSNESS

This brings us back to brains and consciousness. Remember that brains are composed of neurons, and that neurophysiologists have a pretty good understanding of what a neuron is and how it works. But now recall that the number of neurons in a human neocortex may be as high as 30 *billion*, and that the number of interactions among them—that is, the number of synapses at which they connect to one another—is vastly greater than that. Given these two simple yet staggering facts, it is not hard to see how brain function, and specifically that complex set of phenomena we know as consciousness, are emergent phenomena—or, perhaps more specifically, emergent properties of the huge collection of neurons contained in each of our brains. Clearly, the thorough understanding of the physiological and electrochemical functioning of any one neuron does not lead to an understanding of how consciousness works. And equally clearly, no one neuron, or two neurons, or ten neurons can be thought of as conscious. But somehow when we put enough of them together, and interconnect them in a sufficiently complex manner, we end up with consciousness. Philosopher Philip Clayton describes the situation succinctly in two passages:

> The large number of integrated neural circuits in the brain constitutes an extremely complicated whole, which thus constrains the behaviour of its component parts and subsystems in very remarkable ways.
>
> [I]t is impossible to describe Mary's decision to stop by the shop on the way home using well-formed equations in physics. The brain is such a complicated physical system that no interesting predictions of Mary's future brain states can be made using physics alone. In order to make any useful predictions at all, one has to take neurons, synapses, and action potentials as given, together with their causal powers, which means that physics is *not* adequate for one's task. In addition, physical laws simply do not pick out the relevant aspects of the world for making sense of Mary's actions. For that one needs not only biological structures and the laws governing their behavior, but also the theories and correlations of the social sciences. . . . [P]hysics cannot even pick out Mary as a well-formed object; Mary the person is not definable within physics.[20]

To summarize, it seems clear that consciousness—no matter how we define it—is an emergent phenomenon that is the result of vast and tremendously complex interactions among neurons. No single neuron is conscious. In fact, I would suggest (although there is probably no way to prove the suggestion) that no single neuron even "knows" that consciousness exists. Single neurons do not "know" much of anything. They either fire or they do not fire. They don't think, plan, dream, or imagine. They don't get angry or fall in love. Yet we humans, whose brains, personalities, and consciousnesses are made up of nothing more than a huge number of these simple cells, do all these things and more.

Aside from being an emergent phenomenon, there are two more things that we can say with some confidence about consciousness. They may seem obvious, but they will prove important as we proceed. First of all, we can comfortably conclude that consciousness is a product of evolution. That is, it seems most highly developed in human beings, less highly developed in lower animals that evolved long before us, and not at all present on our planet prior to the appearance here of life. Using the rough chronology of cosmic development laid out earlier in this chapter, this means that the very first time anything approaching consciousness might be said to have appeared (on Earth, at least) during the 13–14 billion year history of the universe is about 700 million years ago, with the appearance of the first neurons. (This is a very liberal estimate, following the extreme position that some form of consciousness begins to appear as soon as neural transmission of any sort is available. In fact, it could easily be argued that real consciousness appeared much later.) That means that there was no consciousness for at least the first 12 billion years of the life of the cosmos, and that its appearance characterizes only the most recent segment of the evolutionary timeline.

The second observation, somewhat less apparent but no less important, is that consciousness as an emergent phenomenon seems closely tied to relationships or interactions between things. In other words, the marvels of human consciousness seem dependent on the interconnections among our neurons. The very existence of the neuron came about (according to the view described by Morowitz, cited above) so that disparate, specialized parts of ever-larger organisms could communicate with one another. A more detailed study of evolution reveals that complex cells evolved when earlier, simpler cells incorporated other cells into themselves, with the result being a new cell type with specialized parts (called organelles) inside it—a level of closer relationship or interaction than the one that existed prior to this evolutionary example of "mergers and acquisitions." If we trace the history of the universe back much farther, to the initial appearance of stars, we find once again that this new phase resulted from the closer interaction between the component parts. In other words, the initial formation of stars resulted from a huge number of hydrogen atoms coming together and interacting, smashing into one another, eventually in a most intense way via fusion reactions where two atoms smash together with sufficient force to fuse their nuclei. So it seems that the evolution of the universe as a whole, and of consciousness as one of its most recent features, moves along as things that were separate come together and interact with one another in increasingly complex ways. The actual mechanism of consciousness—that is to say, what really happens in my brain when in the midst of an icy winter storm I think back nostalgically to a lazy summer evening, lying on a blanket at an outdoor concert and drinking chilled white wine—remains an almost total mystery to contemporary neuroscience. But without knowing the details of the mechanism, I believe we can say these three things with confidence:

1. Consciousness is an emergent phenomenon. It is more than the sum of the parts that generate it and cannot be fully understood or predicted by understanding those parts.
2. Consciousness is a product of evolution, and a relatively recent product at that. For most of the history of the universe, there is no reason for us to suspect that consciousness existed, at least based on what we know about the planet on which we live.
3. Consciousness is largely a function of the interactions and interconnections among a very, *very* large number of neurons.

Keep these three observations in mind. They will be crucial as we move forward in our musings about how—if at all—we might think of God as a conscious, sentient entity.

NOTES

1. These distinctions have long been recognized by Jewish philosophy. Medieval thinkers often divided all things into four categories: (1) *domem*, or "silent" (i.e., inanimate things such as minerals); (2) *tzo-me-ach*, or growing (but related to the word *tzemach*, meaning "a plant"); (3) *chai*, alive, meaning animal life; and (4) *m'dabber*, or speaking, referring to the "highest" (since the categories are clearly understood to be hierarchical) form—that is, human.

2. Douglas Hofstadter, *I Am a Strange Loop* (New York: Basic Books, 2007), chap. 1, and especially p. 19.

3. See, for example, Gerald M. Edelman and Giulio Tononi, *A Universe of Consciousness: How Matter Becomes Imagination* (New York: Basic Books, 2000), 102–104 and index.

4. Whether or not animals have higher-order consciousness is still unclear. A good deal of research now suggests that many primates do. According to Florida Atlantic University psychologist David Bjorklund:

> Mirror recognition has been used as a sign of self-awareness. Monkeys exposed to mirrors certainly look in them and seem to find them fascinating, but this alone does not imply self-recognition. To test for self-recognition, scientists use the "mark test" in which a mark is placed on an animal's forehead, without them knowing it. Now when animals look in the mirror, will they realize that the image they see with the strange mark on the forehead is them? If they do, they will touch their own foreheads. If they do not, they will touch the mirror. Human children beginning about 18-months of age "pass" this test (that is, touch their foreheads), as do chimpanzees and orangutans, but at an older age. Most gorillas seem not to understand that they are looking at themselves in the mirror, and, to my knowledge, no monkey, even the very bright capuchin, "pass" this test. So, to come to the point, it is likely that capuchin monkeys who see themselves in the mirror do not know that they are looking at their reflection.

Scientific American Frontiers, http://www.pbs.org/saf/1108/hotline/hbjorklund.htm, accessed 8/14/2014.

The Brain, The Mind, and Consciousness 35

5. This is a vastly oversimplified description of the neuron, a basic "schematic" that will suffice for our consideration of the essential nature of consciousness. The interested reader can pursue a much fuller knowledge in any good introductory neuroscience textbook.

6. "Primitive" is a highly loaded word that is often assiduously avoided when speaking, for example, about human cultures. Here, however, it refers to the fact that evolutionary biologists believe that various brain structures have evolved in a particular sequence and that the mechanisms responsible for primary consciousness are controlled by the oldest parts, rather than the more recently evolved parts, of the brain. We modern humans, whose brains contain the most recently evolved features, still have the older, more "primitive" structures as well.

7. Jeff Hawkins, *On Intelligence* (New York: Henry Holt and Co., 2004), 43. Note, however, that more recently published articles suggest that the number may be as small as 16 billion. See, for example, Suzana Herculano-Houzel, "The Human Brain in Numbers: A Linearly Scaled-up Primate Brain," *Frontiers in Human Neuroscience*, 09 November, 2009, doi: 10.3389/neuro.09.031.2009. This discrepancy in estimates of numbers provides a sense of how new the field of brain research is and how rapidly it changes.

8. Hawkins, *On Intelligence*, 133.

9. The following chronology is based on Carl Sagan, *The Dragons of Eden* (New York: Ballantine Books, 1977), 14–16, and Harold Morowitz, *The Emergence of Everything* (New York: Oxford University Press, 2002), 109. As a chronological guide it is approximate, not precise. But even if some events are off by a bit, it gives us a sense of sequence and rough time scale.

10. Morowitz, *The Emergence of Everything*, 99–101.

11. Henry M. McHenry, "Human Evolution," in *Evolution: The First Four Billion Years*, ed. Michael Ruse and Joseph Travis (Cambridge, MA: Belknap Press of Harvard University Press, 2009), 256.

12. This entire description is based on what is known about the development of life and consciousness on Earth. It is possible that this developmental process occurred earlier in the history of the universe in a different galaxy, but since there is still no evidence of extraterrestrial life, in even a rudimentary form, I restrict these observations to what we know, that is, to our planet.

13. Daniel Dennett, *Consciousness Explained* (Boston: Little, Brown and Co., 1991), 17, 39, 107, and elsewhere.

14. The debate between dualism and its various competing philosophical systems is huge and complex, and is matched by a vast literature. My goal here is only to sketch out a very brief outline. The interested reader is urged to consult any general work on the philosophy of mind for more depth and detail.

15. *The American Heritage Dictionary of the English Language, Fourth Edition*, s.v. "Analysis."

16. The concept of emergence was first described in the early twentieth century, or even earlier, but did not begin to develop in its current form until the second half of the twentieth century. On the early history of the idea, see Philip Clayton, *Mind and Emergence: From Quantum to Consciousness* (New York: Oxford University Press, 2006), chap. 1.

17. The word "higher" may cause discomfort in some readers who have been conditioned to bristle at evaluative terms. It is meant to convey the sense that, in the building of a structure (say, a house) we start at the bottom (the foundation) and build layer upon layer, ever higher, with each layer's stability resting on the layer beneath it. That biology is a "higher" level than chemistry simply means that the rules and elements of chemistry underlie the rules and elements of biology, as the parts of a home's basement underlie the parts of its first floor.

18. Morowitz, *The Emergence of Everything*, 27, 48–53.

19. The details of the process described here are unique to "first-generation" stars. As these stars reach the end of their lifespans and explode, they eject the new, heavier elements out into the universe. Second-generation stars are made up of a wider array of initial elements, including hydrogen, helium, and the other, heavier elements created inside, then spewed out by, the first-generation stars.

20. Clayton, *Mind and Emergence*, 51–53.

Chapter Three

The Emergence of God

Let us pause here to recall where we began. I have come to feel most comfortable with an understanding of God as the complex set of natural laws, forces, and principles that have given rise to the universe in which we live, make it a place of structure instead of a place of randomness, and control its development and govern its behavior. This notion of God, not so different from that of Einstein or Spinoza, is powerful and awesome. It takes our breath away as we gape at the majesty of a mighty mountain or a flaming sunset. It makes us feel small and insignificant by contrast with the vastness of the galaxy. It is a God to whom we can easily say, *"Ma rabu ma'asekha Adonai* [How great are your works, Eternal One!]."[1] The trouble is that this sense of God does not seem to be of a conscious, thinking, feeling Self, one who can plan, choose, wonder, love, or get angry. The principles and forces of Nature are laws but they are not a Lawgiver in the traditional sense. They govern us absolutely but they are not a Ruler in any traditional religious sense. Nevertheless, I still cling to—and cherish—a religious tradition that is critically dependent on human beings having an interactive relationship with a God who thinks, feels, and makes moral judgments. If my sense of God is correct, and if that sense does not permit me to believe that God is conscious, then I must either discard or creatively think my way around much of Jewish tradition.

Now I am perfectly comfortable discarding—or thinking my way around—small, discrete elements of tradition. Doing so is an old and important part of the tradition itself. A simple example is how the rabbis of the Talmud dealt with capital punishment. The Torah expresses complete comfort with the death penalty, prescribing it for adultery, blasphemy, murder, violation of Shabbat, and more. Apparently, the rabbis felt uncomfortable with it, however, and so they encumbered its implementation with a large number of highly demanding rules of evidence and judicial procedure, making it virtually impossible ever to execute a criminal. Thus they were able to maintain the tradition intact without actually supporting, approving of, or engaging in a traditionally sanctioned practice with which they disagreed.

There are many other examples of the tradition reinterpreting pieces of itself virtually out of existence. But completely discarding any sense of God as a Conscious Self strikes me as going too far. It leaves us with so little of what qualifies as traditional Jewish religion that the result would be nearly unrecognizable. God's self is simply too large, too prominent, and too central an element of our texts, our rituals, and our collective memory for me to feel comfortable excising it. So the question before us here is whether there is a way in which we might be able to use the insights of modern science to imagine a conscious God.

THE PROPOSAL ON ONE FOOT

Based on the observations of the previous chapter, I now want to propose a rational way to think of God as a conscious, sentient entity with which (or, we may come to feel comfortable saying, with whom) we can speak, interact, and so on. I propose that we begin with a notion of God as natural law, as stated above. For the first roughly 13 billion or so years of the history of the cosmos, those laws expressed themselves in terms that we would recognize as physics and chemistry. They produced the universe itself and populated it with a huge number of stars, planets, comets, galaxies, and so on. Regarding that time period I still feel comfortable with my sense that God was essentially nonpersonal, nonsentient, and inanimate. Then in the most recent somewhat-less-than-a-billion years, those natural processes gave rise to life here on Earth (and quite likely elsewhere as well).[2] If the previous 13 billion years featured God-as-physics-and-chemistry, this more recent epoch has added God-as-biology to the picture. In the most recent portion of this time period,[3] the evolution of life has led to consciousness of varying levels in life forms, culminating in the extraordinary level of consciousness—that is, higher-order consciousness—experienced by us *Homo sapiens* every day.

Now remember that consciousness, as I have described it, is the emergent property of a huge number of neurons in the neocortex being interconnected in an enormous number of combinations and permutations. We know from our own experience that one of the things that humans do by nature is interact. First by speech, then later by the written word in its myriad forms, we as a species spend most of our time connecting, communicating, and cooperating with fellow human beings. That is to say, the world for at least the last 100,000 years has included a growing number of conscious individuals who interact and interconnect with each other. So here is my proposal, in its simplest form:

> Let us think of the consciousness of God as the emergent property of all the conscious individuals who exist (and who ever have existed) interconnecting with one another.

Let's unpack that simple statement a bit. What I am proposing is an analogy: What an individual neuron is to my consciousness, an individual conscious self is to God's consciousness. If neurons are the units that make up my consciousness, then conscious selves are the units that make up God's consciousness. Just as human consciousness appears and grows as a function of the increasing interconnectedness of our individual neurons, God's consciousness appears and grows as a function of the increasing interconnectedness of conscious human individuals. This analogy has several important ramifications. Just as my consciousness is not located in any one particular place, but is the emergent result of—and coextensive with—the huge complexity of the interactions among my neurons, so God's consciousness is not located in one particular place, but is the emergent result of—and coextensive with—the interactions among all human (and other conscious) beings.[4]

My proposal also draws a distinction between two facets of God's existence. I have argued all along that God is the label we give to the complex set of natural laws that govern the existence of the universe. This facet of God's existence is at least as old as the universe—that is, at least 14 billion or so years old.[5] The facet of God's existence that we would identify as God's consciousness, however, is a rather recent development, having come into existence during perhaps only the last few hundred million years. One may be tempted to interpret this notion as a form of mind-body dualism. Am I suggesting that God has a body that is physical and a mind that is, in Descartes's terms, nonphysical (i.e., "mental")? I would reject such an interpretation. Emergence does not posit that mind is a qualitatively different substance from that which makes up the physical world. Rather, its claim is that an emergent phenomenon is the result of a particular level of interactive complexity among physical processes that leads to the existence of a new level of process. Thus the Internet is not some mysterious nonphysical thing, as distinct from the hard physicality of my desktop computer. Rather, it is a new level of thing, brought into existence by the interconnectedness of billions of computers just like mine.

Similarly, we might consider the process by which a single human being comes into existence. We know that conception—that is, the process by which sperm and egg unite and cell division begins—marks the beginning of what will develop into an individual human being. Yet the first neurons do not appear until about the fifth week of fetal development, with the first synapses appearing shortly thereafter. Given current technology, it is impossible to know exactly when the fetus begins to have anything that we might label as "conscious experience." But based on my fundamental assumption that consciousness is a product of neuronal and synaptic activity, it certainly cannot be before the fifth week (and probably begins much later, as more and more neurons and synapses develop, since emergent consciousness depends on the existence of a very large number of neurons). That means, minimally, that for at least the first month of gestation—and probably more—the fetus is not conscious. By analogy, I am arguing that for the first roughly 13 billion years of God's development, God was not conscious.

Let's look at this idea from another perspective. We do not assume that consciousness is an absolute or necessary characteristic of being human. Even though it is the *usual* state of humanness, we recognize that a person who is comatose, or who has received general anesthesia, is still a person. We are somewhat uncomfortable about assuming the full humanness of a person who is thought to be permanently unconscious—as, for example, in the case of a patient who is brain dead but whose body continues to be kept alive by means of technological intervention. But even here our discomfort is still only partial; that is to say, we are by no means certain that the permanent loss of consciousness renders an individual either no longer human or no longer alive. That is why medical decisions about whether to terminate life-support measures in such a case are such agonizing ethical dilemmas. And even when a person has died, we still do not imagine that she has lost all her personhood. If we believed that, we would not go to such lengths to care for our dead, bury them respectfully, and maintain and visit their graves. The point is that we *can* imagine the notion of "person" without consciousness, despite the fact that the usual state of "person-ness" does involve consciousness. In a similar fashion, I am suggesting that we can imagine God without consciousness, even though human beings for the most part have experienced God as conscious. And just as the human embryo in its first phase of gestation but before the development of neurons is still a marvelous thing, so it is not hard to think of God—in the first 13 billion years of cosmic history—as accomplishing a tremendous amount, driving the development of stars, galaxies, and galactic clusters without being conscious.

A PHILOSOPHICAL REVOLUTION

I must be candid here about the heterodox nature of what I am proposing. For a good deal of Jewish history, most mainstream Jewish philosophers have made certain assumptions about God that I am rejecting. This is the case for two assumptions in particular. The first is that God is eternally unchanging. That is, God's full nature has always been fully present in God. God has not developed and does not develop. Or, to put it another way, in the distinction between things that are "potential" and things that are "actual," there is no potential in God. That is, there are no possibilities in God for characteristics or abilities or attributes that are not currently realized but that might become realized at some future point. Everything that God ever could be, God is, always has been, and always will be. My proposal that God has developed consciousness as an added feature of God's existence is a clear rejection of that ancient assumption. This is revolutionary in the context of the history of Jewish philosophy, especially to the extent that Jewish philosophy has been profoundly influenced by the thought of Aristotle. But to me it seems clear. Our universe is characterized at all times by change. We live in a dynamic reality, not a static one. All things, from the weird, quantum world of the subatomic to the massive world of the super-galactic, are constantly in motion and in a state of becoming. Physicists struggle to achieve temperatures near absolute zero, that state of perfect cold at which all motion—even at the molecular and atomic levels—stops, but their efforts are so far unsuccessful. In the world of modern cosmology, the very history of the universe is a history of motion and becoming, from the first instant of the Big Bang (when our universe was born in a massive outflowing of pure energy) to the early twentieth century discovery that the universe is constantly expanding. Modern science has taught us that even things that seem permanent and unchanging, like the great mountains or the emptiness of outer space, are actually in a constant state of change, development, and intense activity. Time itself may be conceived as nothing more than a way of measuring change. And the fact of biology, of life itself, is completely characterized by change, with birth, growth, decay, and death being the familiar landmarks on a path that is constantly becoming.

If such is the nature of all reality, it makes no sense to me to assume that God is unique among all elements of reality as a static and never-changing entity. If I were to believe that God is the *only* static, unchanging force or entity in a universe wholly characterized by change, motion, energy, and becoming, I would have to believe that God could never have anything to do with the universe. For as soon as an unchanging and static force were to have any contact or interaction with a constantly changing and developing universe, the unchanging force would be changed. This paradox has in fact bothered Jewish thinkers for centuries. For a rationalist like Maimonides, the notion that God is perfect must mean that God does not *need* anything, for to need something means that one's current state is less perfect than it would be if one had the needed thing. So to imagine that God needs anything (even, say, human obedience or devotion) would imply that without these things God is less complete than God would be with them. That is what need is all about. So God cannot need us or anything else.

Such a God, independent of all things, may be an interesting notion for philosophers to contemplate, but seems to me not terribly compelling for religious human beings who at the very least wonder about God's impact on the world, and at the most desperately seek *interaction with* God.[6] According to much of Jewish tradition, the seeking is mutual, as we see in the Talmudic assertion that "the Holy Blessed One desires the heart."[7] In short, it only makes sense to me, as a person committed to the value of religious life, to think of God as interacting with reality and thus, like the rest of the universe, as being in a constant state of change—or, in other words, of constantly becoming. This way of thinking certainly fits well with the biblical understanding of God. In the first verse of the Torah, God "began to create" the universe (Gen. 1:1). Later God "took note of Sarah" and allowed her to bear a child (Gen. 21:1). Later still God "heard the outcry" of the enslaved Hebrews and "remembered His covenant with Abraham, with Isaac, and with Jacob" (Ex. 2:24). In these and a large number of other examples, God chose to act in a particular way at a particular time. Such discrete acts are signs of change. Before God took note of Sarah, God had not taken note of her. The "taking note" was a change. Thus the biblical portrayal of God is not at all concerned with God's eternal immutability. It was only later that Jewish philosophers, under the influence of Greek thought, became committed to this notion.[8]

With regard to my rejection of the traditional belief in God's unchanging nature, there is a further curious result of thinking about God as emergent. I have argued that consciousness is one of the most recent features to emerge as the result of the evolutionary processes that underlie the development of the universe. But just as it would be illogical and arrogant to imagine that evolution has reached its end or its pinnacle with us, and therefore that there can and will be no further evolution beyond human beings, so it would be similarly illogical and arrogant to imagine that the emergent phenomenon or force that we think of as God's consciousness is the end—the last level of emergence that will ever come to be. Such an assumption would be the equivalent of an imaginary thinking being 450 million years ago observing the appearance in the Earth's oceans of sharks and, being suitably impressed with their design, structure, and grace, assuming that they are the "crown of creation" and that it can't get any better, any more complex or sublime, than that! It is humbling and mind boggling to realize that the current emergent state of what we know as God's consciousness *cannot* be the ultimate emergence. We are incapable of imagining any further emergences. Yet it makes no sense to conclude therefore that there can and will be no future levels, that emergence has reached the zenith.

The second fundamental assumption of ancient tradition that I reject is that "God is One" means, among other things, that God is not composed of any parts, that God's unity is a single irreducible oneness that cannot be composed of any smaller elements. According to this traditional view, God is ultimately and radically simple, not complex. But according to my proposal, God's consciousness can be thought of as separate from God's existence, since God's consciousness is a relatively recent feature of God's existence—an "add-on" of the last less-than-a-billion years. As such, God is composed of at least two parts: the physicality expressed in the development of the universe according to a complex and orderly set of physical laws for the first several billion years of our universe's life, and the consciousness that has developed only in the last several hundred million years. We can easily imagine the earth without consciousness or life (in fact, this is a possible scenario with which we have become altogether too familiar in the decades since the first use of nuclear weapons) and we can imagine the universe without—that is, prior to—these features. As I observed above, we can even imagine human beings without consciousness, temporarily (as when under anesthesia) or permanently (as when dead). Why then should we not be able to imagine God in a state prior to the development of divine consciousness? If we can imagine this preconscious divine state, then God's current state is *more complex* than it was before the advent of consciousness.

Even reasoning solely from the logic dictated by observing our universe, it makes no sense to think of God as being ultimately simple. This argument is similar to the one (sketched above) against God's being unchanging or static. Our universe has been characterized by ever-increasing complexity. A star is more complex than a hydrogen atom, life is more complex than the absence of life, multi-celled living creatures are more complex than single-celled organisms, a symphony is more complex than a simple tune played on a reed flute. Just as I cannot believe in a static God as a part of an always-dynamic universe, I cannot believe in a simple God in an increasingly complex universe. When our tradition thinks of God as utterly unique, I cannot imagine it means that God is unique in a way that makes God *less* than the rest of reality, but only that God is unique in a way that makes God *more* than all other parts of reality. And for me a static God in a dynamic universe, or a simple God in a complex universe, would indeed be less. I would even go so far as to say that God is the ultimate in both complexity and dynamism, and therein lie two elements of God's uniqueness.

HUMANS VERSUS GOD: A FALSE DICHOTOMY

The idea of God's consciousness as an emergent phenomenon has numerous implications when considered against the backdrop of a long history of Jewish thoughts and beliefs about God. It suggests a blurring of the distinction between the divine and the human aspects of Judaism. In fact, such fuzziness of the boundary between the human and the divine, though it may seem entirely modern and anti-traditional, has some support in the Jewish past. We see hints of such support clearly in a strange rabbinic text: "Said Rabbi Joshua ben Levy: Scripture, Mishnah and Talmud, laws [*halakhot*], legends [*aggadot*], and even that which an expert student will teach in the presence of his teacher in the future, was already said to Moses on Sinai."[9] This is an example of a class of rabbinic statements intended to address the question of what Moses actually heard from God at Sinai. The question itself is an interesting one, for it reveals a fundamental uncertainty in the worldview of the rabbis regarding what the process of revelation involves.

The rabbis believed that the Torah was revealed to Moses on Sinai—of that we can be quite sure. What they were not certain of was what that simple statement meant. Did such a belief require that one view the entire Torah, every word of it, as having been spoken by God to Moses during the forty days and nights that Moses spent on the mountain? Or might it be enough to imagine that only some limited portion had been revealed directly, and that the rest was the product of either human legislation or human interpretation? Some claim that only the Ten Commandments were actually spoken out loud by God, while others claim that only the first two commandments—or even only the first commandment—was spoken. In a famous and oft-quoted maximalist (or minimalist, depending on where you stand) view, one Hasidic teacher even claimed that all that Moses actually heard was the first letter of the first word of the first commandment. The commandment is "I am Adonai your God, who brought you out of the land of Egypt." The first word of the commandment is *Anokhi*, meaning "I" or "I am,"[10] and the first letter is *aleph*, which is silent. Such a view would seem to suggest that most of the content of revelation comes from the human listeners instead of from the divine speaker. The extreme of this position is the basis upon which Franz Rosenzweig commented on the revelation at Mount Sinai in Exodus chapters 19 and 20, as quoted by Emil Fackenheim: "'He [i.e. God] came down' [onto Mount Sinai]—this already concludes the revelation; 'He spoke' is the beginning of interpretation, and certainly 'I am.'"[11] In the same way that the modern literary theory of deconstruction suggests that the meaning of a text comes mostly, if not entirely, from the reader rather than from the author, this view of revelation sees most, if not all, of the specific content of revelation (as opposed, perhaps, to the experience of revelation) as coming from the recipient rather than the Revealer.

By contrast, the statement quoted here in the name of Rabbi Joshua Ben Levy suggests a different extreme position. The entirety of Scripture, he says, was spoken to Moses on Sinai. Not just the Torah, but the other portions of the Bible as well, apparently including even those many parts seen by the tradition as having been authored by humans. For example, the traditional view is that King Solomon wrote both Ecclesiastes and the Song of Songs, while King David wrote the Psalms, and so on. But the word used by Joshua

Ben Levy is *mikra,* the most generic and inclusive word for "scripture." This extreme claim, however, is only the beginning. He goes on to claim that other texts, texts that form the heart of the Oral Law and are typically viewed as being of completely human origin ("Mishnah and Talmud, laws [*halakhot*], legends [*aggadot*]") were also spoken to Moses on Sinai. In a final flourish of audacity, he then adds the notion that even material not yet produced, "that which an expert student will teach in the presence of his teacher in the future," was also included in the revelation to Moses. What does this mean? A typical interpretation sees this text as describing a process where revelation comes initially in a tight little package that then must be unpacked in a centuries-long process. This unpacking, which seems to us to be a human activity of innovation but is really just an uncovering or decoding of what was in the original package, takes the rest of human history to complete. Thus the new idea that will be raised by a student in a classroom next week is no more new than the dinosaur bone that is still buried and undiscovered on a farm in Iowa but that may be dug up by a paleontologist next week. Both the idea and the bone have been there for a long time, waiting to be unearthed.

I would propose a different reading of Rabbi Joshua Ben Levy's claim. I suggest that we not see the phrase "was already said to Moses on Sinai" as denoting a particular moment in time—that is, as specifying that the material in question was literally revealed to Moses on Sinai some thousands of years ago—but rather that we take the phrase to mean "is part of divine revelation." Here "divine revelation" means that which God tells us in an ongoing process. That the process is ongoing is important. In contradistinction to the more widespread notion that the revelation happened all at once, but that it came to us in so tightly packed and encoded a form that it will take us all of human history to untangle it, "ongoing revelation" means that the actual process of getting new revelation from God continues in every generation, up to and including our own and those yet to come. If God's consciousness, God's Self, is the emergent result of the massively complex interconnectedness among all other selves and consciousnesses, then every time human beings interact in a complex way their collective voice is, in a real sense, the voice of God. It makes no sense to ask, with the tradition, "Which part of the result came from God and which part was the result of human interpretation?" The simple distinction between the two has dissolved in our understanding that "God" is what results from the interaction.

We turn now to another Talmudic text, a relatively well known one this time, that will provide a different nuance to our understanding of how the concept of an emergent God undercuts the traditional distinction between humans and the divine:

> Rav Judah said in the name of Rav: When Moses ascended on high [to receive the Torah] he found the Holy Blessed One sitting and tying decorative crowns

on the letters. Said Moses, "Sovereign of the universe, who is keeping you back?" God answered, "At the end of many generations there will be a man named Akiva ben Joseph who will derive heaps and heaps of laws from every part of every letter." "Sovereign of the universe," said Moses, "permit me to see him." God said, "Turn around." Moses turned and found himself in the eighth row [at the back of Rabbi Akiva's academy]. He was not able to understand what they were saying. He was overwhelmed by weakness and despair. Then, when they came to a certain subject, the students said to Rabbi Akiva, "How do you know this law?" He replied, "It is a law given to Moses at Sinai." Moses was comforted.[12]

The text is a midrash, a somewhat fanciful, imagined description of what it might have been like when Moses climbed Mount Sinai to receive the revelation of the Torah from God. As such it is a typical vehicle by which the rabbis expressed their theological or philosophical beliefs. This particular midrash is an extraordinarily rich piece about rabbinic power and humility, God's role as Revealer, and—in the continuation of the text, not reproduced here—some very thorny questions about the limitations on God's power and justice. But for the purpose of the present discussion, I want to comment on just a few of its features.

At the start of the tale, Moses finds God engaging in some curious behavior—namely, tying crowns (the decorative calligraphic flourishes[13] that are assumed by the text's author to convey secret meaning) on the letters. When he asks God to explain this surprising activity, God explains that the crowns on the letters encode textual information that will be decoded by Rabbi Akiva, one of the premier scholars of the early second century CE. Moses expresses a desire to see such a great master of Torah interpretation and God responds by transporting Moses many hundreds of years into his own future and depositing him in the eighth row of seats in Akiva's academy. (The eighth row is significant because the ancient rabbinic academy placed the most advanced students in the front and the newest ones in the back.) Moses listens to the discussion but cannot understand it, presumably because the level of discussion has progressed far beyond the simple meaning of the written Torah (which Moses knows) to include details of oral interpretive tradition, which he does not know and has not anticipated. Finally, the students ask Rabbi Akiva about the origin of a tradition and the teacher responds, "It is a law given to Moses at Sinai," thereby making Moses feel a little better.

The tale is usually understood as suggesting that the seeds of all later innovations and legal interpretations of the Torah were included in the initial revelation to Moses in the desert, and that the later human (that is, rabbinic) role is less innovation and more decoding of that which is hidden in the original text. Such an understanding legitimates rabbinic interpretation, even when it seems clearly to be innovative, as merely "discovering" that which

God concealed in the system from the outset. But I would suggest, in keeping with the notion of God's consciousness as the emergent result of the interaction among human consciousnesses, that what is going on in Akiva's academy is something more straightforward. In fact, Akiva and his students *are* innovating, legislating, and breaking new ground. They are adding to the content of the revelation at Sinai. This fact alone is enough to make Moses feel queasy; after all, the revelation that he heard included the verse "Take care to fulfill every thing that I command you; do not add to it or take away from it."[14] But Akiva claims, in response to his students' query, that these innovations are part and parcel of the process of divine revelation, "a law given to Moses at Sinai." This is not meant to suggest that the particular law being discussed at that moment in the class was included, somehow buried deep under the surface, in the content that Moses brought down from the mountain. Rather, the innovative process of hammering out new laws, or new legal interpretations, *in the interactive community of the academy* is part of the process of divine revelation because God's consciousness—God's very presence—is what happens when human beings put their heads together.

THE INDISPENSABLE COMMUNITY

These last two passages—that is, Rabbi Joshua ben Levy's statement about the status of everything that an expert student will teach in the presence of his teacher in the future, and the story of Moses in Rabbi Akiva's academy—suggest that the rabbis of the Talmudic era were already focused on, and had begun to intuit the deep importance of, communal interaction. Although they would never have thought of it or expressed it in the radical terms that I am arguing—namely, that God's consciousness *is* what emerges from the interaction of human consciousnesses—they had a strong sense of the value of communal interaction, especially (though not entirely, as we shall see in a moment) the intellectual interaction of the academy.

Even the well-known Talmudic story of Aknai's oven makes this point: The opinions of a single individual—in that case Rabbi Eliezer—cannot possibly take precedence over the voices of the majority of his colleagues, even when Rabbi Eliezer's view is supported by a heavenly voice.[15] What Rabbi Eliezer is doing smacks of the biblical style of divine-human relationship, in which God for the most part was portrayed as speaking to a single individual. If we think about almost any of the biblical narratives of divine communication, the model is always the same: God speaks to Noah about the flood, not to the whole human race. God speaks to Abraham, whose job it will be to spread the message of the covenant. God speaks to Moses (and occasionally to Aaron) and it is their responsibility to confront both the Egyptians and their own people. And certainly the prophets all functioned in a context in which it was assumed that God spoke to individuals and that those individuals were tasked with transmitting God's word to the people. This is the case so much so, in fact, that in one memorable instance when God *does* speak to the whole community—namely, when God gives them the Ten Commandments—the people respond with fear and beg Moses to be God's messenger: "*You* speak to us . . . and we will obey. But let not God speak to us, lest we die!"[16]

But the early rabbis had a sense that this sort of divine, one-on-one revelation was over and had been replaced by the divine voice as reflected in human interaction. This intuitive sense extended even beyond the study house, as we see in the following rabbinic text:

> Any time ten people enter a synagogue the *Shekhinah* [divine presence] is with them, as it is written, "God stands in the congregation of God" (Ps. 82:1). And whence do we know it even regarding three who are judging? It is written, "In the midst of the judges He judges" (*ibid.*). And whence do we know it even regarding two? It is written, "Then they that feared the Lord spoke with one another" (Mal. 3:16). And whence do we know it regarding even one person? It is written, "In every place in which I cause My name to be mentioned I will come to you" (Ex. 20:24).[17]

Here the claim is being made that the Shekhinah, or "Presence of God," can be found wherever the Jewish people engage in what might loosely be termed "sacred activity," although frankly it is not clear exactly what the author of the text imagined the "two people" and "one person" to be doing. In its original context, the passage was probably providing an answer to the question that plagued Jewish thinkers following the traumatic destruction of the Temple by the Romans in 70 CE—namely, "Where is God?" Without the Temple, which had housed the divine presence for almost five centuries,[18] the rabbis wondered where God was located. Did God choose to stay at the site of the destroyed Temple? Or had God chosen to abandon that holy site and remain with the people in their exile? This passage, along with others scattered throughout rabbinic literature, claims that God insists on staying with the people. Wherever they might gather, that is where God would choose to cause the Shekhinah to dwell.

I am suggesting a different interpretation of the passage. Rather than see it as a vote in the debate over whether God chose geography or sociology (that is, the holy land or the holy people) to define God's post-destruction place of residence, I see it as an expression of a growing rabbinic sense that God's presence appears where people interact with one another—that is, that the Shekhinah grows out of (*emerges* from) the functioning of community. Let me be very clear here: The rabbis themselves would never have entertained the thought that God's presence exists as the emergent result of the interaction among human selves. That is my claim, not theirs. But they clearly have a sense that God's presence is invoked by, or attracted to, such interactions among Jews.

This belief is certainly a part of the ancient legal requirement that there be a *minyan*, or quorum of ten adult Jewish men,[19] in order to conduct a number of liturgical and ritual events. These include the recitation of *Barkhu*, the call to prayer before the blessings of *Sh'ma Yisrael* ("Hear O Israel") in the morning and evening service; the leader's repetition of the *Tefilah*, the main part of the service; the recitation of Kaddish; the public reading of the Torah and Haftarah with their attendant blessings; and more. This requirement suggests that it is impossible or forbidden to engage totally with God except in community. The requirement of a minyan suggests that the divine presence is there when the community gathers, but does not appear for just one individual, or even for nine. Using the language of God as emergent, we could say that the token interaction of even a small community of ten allows a fleeting glimpse into the nature of God's Self as the emergent result of the complex interconnectedness of a very large number of human consciousnesses. This makes sense in light of the concern in the medieval and modern legal codes about the permissibility of counting in a minyan one who has fallen asleep, or one who is mad[20] or a deaf-mute.[21] The impairment of such individuals is specifically around issues of interaction. There is no doubt whatsoever that they are full-fledged human beings, but they have limited abilities to connect with others. Thus their ineligibility to make up a minyan reflects no sense that they are less than human, but rather a sense that they are humans who cannot interact properly with others. To use the emergent analogy of the Internet, these persons are like computers with little or no capacity to connect to other computers.

If a minimal community (a minyan) of interacting consciousnesses can give us a fleeting glimpse into God's consciousness, then being with a very large community might give us an even clearer sense of this. Such is the implication of the Talmudic statement attributed to R. Chanina ben Ika that when one sees a crowd of 600,000 Jews one should recite the blessing "Blessed are You, Eternal our God, Knower of secrets."[22] I suggest that this blessing be interpreted to mean that when a very large crowd gathers, the emergent result is the appearance of a mind that can indeed know secrets— that is, the Mind of God.

HUMANISM AND THEISM: SURVEYING THE BORDER

Earlier in this chapter, I made the claim that the traditional Jewish debate about the relative roles of human beings and God, especially in revelation and law, are based on a false distinction. If what we identify as God's consciousness or Self is the emergent result of the interconnectedness among other (primarily human) consciousnesses, then it is especially difficult—perhaps even impossible—to isolate the point where divine input ends and human input begins. The fact that Jewish tradition relies heavily upon the notion of religious life in community makes this clean distinction even more difficult. If there were ample room in Jewish history for hermits, or lone scholars toiling in isolation, we might be able to find the line between God and humankind. But because Jewish sacred tradition places such value on, for example, prayer in community (the requirement for a minyan) and study in community (the tradition of the *beit midrash*, or communal house of study where students discuss and argue the fine points of legal texts in a cacophony of interaction), the line between God's presence and communal interaction becomes hopelessly blurry.

The indistinctness of the boundary leads inevitably to a challenge: Isn't what I have proposed really just humanism, a simple rejection of the existence of an independent God who is really "out there" somewhere and can really function in the world and in our lives? Is this not really just a belief that humans are the sole actors on the stage of history? My emphatic answer is no. To understand why we must go back to the concept of emergence for a moment. By definition, an emergent phenomenon comes into existence as the result of complex interaction among a set of preexisting elements. But once it has appeared, the emergent phenomenon has an existence that is separate from—and on a higher level than—the component parts that comprise it. The market is an emergent phenomenon resulting from the interaction among a large number of buyers and sellers. If you were to take away *all* the buyers and sellers, the market would disappear. But as long as the buyers and sellers are there, and they continue buying and selling in complex and interactive ways, the market exists as an entity that is separate from them and that can (and does) have influence over them. To claim that "there is no market, just buyers and sellers," would be to ignore core principles of economics, not to mention simple observations of reality.

Similarly, God's Self is a real and separate entity that exists independently of us and can—and often does—affect us in numerous ways. Thus, even though God's consciousness is totally dependent on our consciousness for its existence (that is, if all conscious life in the universe were suddenly to disappear, then God's consciousness would also disappear), nevertheless God's Selfhood exists. It's not "just humans."

Most humanists would claim that all of reality can be described and (at least theoretically) explained with reference to nature, science, and rational processes, without recourse to God. I would, in fact, agree almost entirely with this claim, but with a small—though crucial—modification: All of reality can be described and (at least theoretically) explained with reference to nature, science, and rational processes, without recourse to supernaturalism. The difference is that *we may reject supernaturalism without rejecting the existence of a real, active God.* Rejecting supernaturalism simply means rejecting the belief that there is a realm beyond, outside, or above nature. But if we assume that "nature" is a label that we apply to all that exists (that is to say, to the universe and the processes that govern its behavior), then nothing is supernatural.

We may think that a phenomenon is supernatural merely because we cannot understand it in a natural way. Imagine, if you will, what the reaction would be if by a trick of time travel we could show an ordinary, moderately intelligent individual of the twelfth century an electric light, an x-ray of a human skull, or a radio. This scenario, an old staple of television and movie comedies, would certainly lead that individual to conclude that the device was supernatural or magical. Given the knowledge of that time, these are understandable conclusions that demonstrate the wisdom of the famous "Third Law" of the late British science fiction writer Arthur C. Clarke: "Any sufficiently advanced technology is indistinguishable from magic." Yet we who use lights, x-rays, and radios regularly know that they are neither supernatural nor magical, but rather are clever inventions that exploit our knowledge of nature to make our lives better. Similarly, in our own era, the label "supernatural" is often applied to things for which there is no immediately apparent explanation. I believe that, in principle at least, most or all of these can and will eventually be explained and understood as natural processes—as is the case with the radio, x-ray, or electric light.

But a more precise use of the word "supernatural" implies an altogether different scenario in which phenomena are divided into two categories: the *natural*, which includes all phenomena caused by, and explainable with reference to, the laws and processes that govern the physical universe; and the *supernatural*, which includes all phenomena that lie outside the natural world. So, for example, we know that the laws of physics absolutely control the motions of celestial bodies, including the earth and the sun. Both the laws and the movement that they control are understood so well that scientists can predict such things as time of sunrise and sunset with tremendous precision, even well into the future. If some force or being could arbitrarily suspend or change those laws, such a force or being would clearly be in the category of the supernatural. A famous example of this occurs in a story from the biblical book of Joshua: Five Amorite kings attacked the town of Giv'on because Giv'on had entered an alliance with Joshua and his Israelite forces. The besieged king of Giv'on sent a message to Joshua asking for help and Joshua came to his aid with all the Israelite soldiers. The Israelites routed the armies of the five Amorite kings, and during the course of the battle we read:

> Joshua then spoke to the Eternal on the day that the Eternal defeated the Amorites before the Israelites. He said, in the sight of all Israel, "O sun at Giv'on and moon in the Valley of Ayalon, stand still!" So the sun stood still

and the moon stopped until a nation had taken vengeance on its enemies. . . .
The sun stopped in mid-course and did not proceed to set for an entire day.[23]

This is truly a story of a supernatural event in which God suspends the natural forces that control the regular and predictable motions of the sun, the earth, and the moon, stopping the passage of time so that the Israelite armies will have more daylight to wage their battle against the Amorite forces. As a true suspension of the laws of nature, this qualifies as supernatural.

Many religious thinkers assume that God *must* be outside the realm of nature. This notion originated in the ancient Jewish rejection of pre-Israelite pagan religions, in which nature—or various elements of nature—was worshipped. The first stirrings of monotheism actively rejected such worship. The sun, moon, stars, oceans, mountains, rivers, fields, trees, and so on were not deities, but were rather creations of the single God whose power was expressed in His creation of nature. Psalm 19 proclaims, "The heavens tell of the glory of God," and the first blessing of the evening service describes God as the one who "orders the stars in their courses in the sky according to His will." God asks Job, "Where were you when I laid the earth's foundations? . . . Have you ever in your life given orders to the morning? . . . Have you ever visited the place where the snow is kept?"[24] It is a logical next step in this argument to claim that the God who created nature can, and from time to time does, intervene in nature and suspend its laws. The only way to imagine a God who created all of nature and who can suspend its workings at will is to conclude that God must be utterly outside of and independent of nature, or in other words that God must be *super*natural.

I am arguing that we may think of God as being God, and being a real entity, while still being *inside* nature—that is, a natural rather than a supernatural God. Some elements of Jewish tradition will certainly bristle at this claim. But what is the real reason for their objection? From the earliest days of Israelite monotheism, it seemed to make no sense to worship a single element of nature over others—that is, to privilege one part of nature over other parts. Sun worship, or moon worship, or sea worship made no sense, since none of these was an absolute power. The sun rules only the day, not the night, and even during the day it can be obscured by clouds. And the moon disappears altogether once a month. As for the sea, although its power is awesome, it is bounded and limited by the shore, and therefore its might is nowhere near absolute. So it is with every other element of nature. Based perhaps on this line of thinking, which was revolutionary in the ancient world, early Israelite thinkers and their Jewish descendants rejected the worship of any part or parts of nature, insisting that only the supreme power that ruled all these other forces was worthy of worship. And any power that ruled all parts of nature had to be outside of nature—that is, outside of the system that it controlled.

This ancient reasoning is compelling and was certainly a crucial step in the evolution of religious thought. But when I claim that God is within nature rather than outside of it, I am not suggesting that God is identical with one particular part of nature. Rather, God is an *expression of* the entire system that we call nature. At its core this claim rests on the rejection of any sense of dualism in understanding the universe. There is not, on the one hand, nature, and on the other hand something or anything else. Rather, the word "nature" is a label for everything that exists and happens in the universe. That includes the processes of stellar, planetary, and biological evolution that have resulted in what is normally referred to as "nature": stars, galaxies, planets, mountains, oceans, and the entire range of living things that we observe in the world. But I also include in the category "nature" human life and all that it produces. That is where my use of the term constitutes a rejection of dualism and a departure from the way the terms "nature" and "natural" are typically used.

It has become quite common in our society to distinguish what is "natural" from what is "unnatural" or "artificial" (or, occasionally, "man-made"). The former category dominates the labels of foodstuffs that are supposed to be beneficial to our health. They proudly proclaim that they are "All Natural!" Sometimes they add, "Nothing Artificial Added." This implies that "natural" is a term appropriately applied only to those things that exist without the intervention of human technology, which is seen as unnatural or artificial and, by implication, dangerous, unhealthful, or bad. Now while I would not dispute the notion that many products of our modern technological creativity are not good for us, I reject the notion that they are unnatural. For them to be unnatural would require us to believe that we, as human beings, are outside of nature—a claim that is clearly false. We are a result of the same evolutionary processes that gave rise to our close cousins the chimpanzees, as well as our more distant cousins the tulips and the earthworms. A slightly more refined version of the claim would be that it is only our *technology* that is outside of nature (that is to say, *un*natural), but this claim is no less misguided. Technology is usually thought of as involving concrete and asphalt, computers and electronics, and the alleged evils of genetically modified crops. But in fact technology also includes *all* uses of tools, *all* agriculture, and *all* activities by which we affect the environment in which we live. As soon as we stopped browsing on whatever edibles the forest provided us by chance, and began to cultivate crops in straight rows, we were using technology. That we now cultivate those straight rows of crops using computer-controlled irrigation, laboratory-synthesized pesticides and fertilizers, and genetically modified seeds does not make the more ancient version of agriculture more *natural*; it only makes it more primitive, less technologically sophisticated. Both the ancient and the modern forms of agriculture are natural, since we—the designers of agriculture—are a part of nature. Some of our technology (at times it seems a great deal of it) may be harmful to the environment in which we live, or to our very lives, but that fact ought not lead us to conclude that it is unnatural. Like it or not, we—including our brains, our technology, our thoughts, and our consciousness—are a part of nature. It is in this sense that I reject the dualistic possibility that there are two realms in the universe, the Natural and the Non- (or Un- or Super-) Natural. And it is in this sense that I am arguing that God, and God's consciousness, are not supernatural, but are a part or a function of nature.

KNOWING GOD

Few of the questions that I have addressed in these pages are new, though some of the answers may seem new, perhaps even revolutionary. But the questions are, for the most part, as ancient as philosophy and religion. And so it is with a question that stands before us now—namely, how is it possible for us to know God?

This question has a venerable history. During his long night of wrestling by the river, Jacob says to the "man" with whom he is struggling (but whom most commentaries understand as God or as an angelic messenger of God), "Tell me your name!" This seems to be a demand for knowledge of the personal identity of the man. The text continues: "He said, 'Why would you ask my name?' and he blessed him there."[25] Again, after the incident of the Golden Calf, Moses asks God to let him see (meaning experience directly, or know) God's glory, but God refuses, saying, "You cannot see My face, for no person shall see Me and live."[26] As a compromise, God shows Moses God's "back" (or perhaps, depending on how one interprets the biblical language, what comes after God). Texts like these suggest that the extent to which humans can know God is limited at best. And in fact, as we look through Jewish literature, we see a widespread belief that humans cannot really know God at all. We are commanded to love God, to obey God, even to imitate God, but there is a strong—if not quite unanimous—sense that we cannot really know God at all.

In light of this ancient view, I want to turn back for a moment to earlier observations about the brain, neurons, and the emergent nature of consciousness. Remember that despite many historical attempts to locate the seat of consciousness in the brain, there is no discrete part of the brain that houses the self. Instead consciousness is the emergent result of massively complex interaction among many billions of neurons. It is reasonable to imagine that no one of those neurons—not even the longest, smartest one—knows that I am a thinking, conscious, aware self. Nevertheless, even though not one of those billions of neurons in my head is aware of the thing called "Me," the "Me" is nothing more than a function of their interconnection.

Here is the paradox: Despite the fact that much of Jewish tradition says that we mere humans cannot know God, and despite the fact that no neuroscientist would ever claim that a neuron can know what it is like to be a conscious, thinking self, I have made the claim that we human beings (who are analogous to the neurons that taken all together make up God's consciousness), can indeed have a sense that there is a "Self" or a consciousness that is God. We humans have a deep sense that God is a conscious Self. Now as paradoxical as this initially appears, it should not be so surprising. For the analogy between an individual human being and a neuron is only a rough, structural analogy.

A neuron is to my entire conscious self what a human self is to God's entire conscious Self. But that's where the similarity ends. Aside from being elements in a tremendously complex emergent phenomenon, the neuron and the human being bear little resemblance to one another. Neurons are relatively simple biological mechanisms that don't do much. Depending on the electrochemical input that they receive, they either fire or they don't. Obviously, even this description is a vast oversimplification, but it is not unjustified when we compare the simple neuron to the human self who thinks, imagines, plans, dreams, implements, evaluates, worries, wonders, loves, hates, gets bored and excited, feels proud and guilty and sympathetic, and is both aware and aware of being aware. The fact that we humans can understand—even in the most rudimentary manner—the very notion of emergence should give us some sense of the huge difference in scale and kind between the complexity and sophistication of a human self and that of a neuron. Those characteristics allow us to be aware that there is "something bigger than us" out there.

On the other hand, if Thomas Nagel tells us that we simply cannot know what it is like to be a bat, then we certainly cannot know at all what it is like to be God. We may imagine that God has a consciousness, a self, and if so we are necessarily limited to imagining that self as somewhat analogous to our own selves. But even as we do so, we are acutely aware that there is no real basis for that imagined analogy. The problem is that we have only one way of being human selves, and that limits us strictly in our ability to imagine what it is like to be other, nonhuman selves. Thus, although our knowledge of God is necessarily quite limited because we cannot possibly know what it is like to be God (notice that the source of the limitation is the logic of Nagel, not a prohibition imposed by God), we can imagine that it is like *something* to be God. And we can know this, despite our inability to really understand what that something is.

The limitation on human imagination and language may have been part of what Maimonides was reacting to when he cautioned us to understand all the anthropomorphic God-language of the Torah—God walking, seeing, hearing, smelling; God's finger, hand, face, back, and so on—as merely figures of speech, not to be thought of as bearing any resemblance to those same words, or their underlying content, when applied to humans. Despite this philosophical warning, we find it virtually impossible *not* to think of God in human terms. When we read Abraham's challenge to God ("Shall the Judge of all the earth not behave justly?"[27]), we cannot help but think of what it is like to be a human judge, even though there is little reason to suspect that what it is like for God to be a judge bears any resemblance to what it is like for people to be judges. As soon as we start to realize that God's judge-ness, or king-ness, or shepherd-ness is completely unlike human versions of these activities, the use of such metaphors begins to lose its effectiveness.

Elsewhere I have proposed that one solution to this problem is to develop new metaphors for God, especially metaphors not drawn from the realm of human experiences. Yet this solution is at best a partial one, since our religious traditions (developed over the course of many centuries) have conditioned us to want and need to think of God and relate to God as a superhuman. And so we are left with the unresolved paradox: Even if we find the notion of emergence to be highly useful in explaining how God's consciousness might function, nevertheless the very nature of emergence—especially the fact that by definition the emergent phenomenon operates according to different rules than those governing its component parts—still leaves us without true access to knowledge of the nature of God. We can know that God does exist, in a real sense, "out there" as a consciousness, and we can even know that it is our collective, interconnected consciousnesses that generate the divine consciousness, but we still cannot know what it is like to *be* God.

BEYOND GOD

Before concluding this sketch of the theological implications of God as emergent, we turn to one final, revolutionary observation. Ancient Jewish belief has held firmly that God is eternal, unchanging, and absolute. And it is clear that the superlatives applied traditionally to God are seen not only as setting God completely apart from (and above) anything or anyone that ever *has* been, but also as setting God apart from (and above) anything that ever will be or could be. According to traditional belief, it is impossible—not just highly unlikely, but *impossible*—for anything to ever eclipse God.

I long ago stopped thinking about God as eternal. When thinking and writing about Jewish belief through the lens of physics some years ago, I came to accept the theory that our universe had a starting point in the finite past with the Big Bang, roughly 14 billion years ago. Now philosophers or theologians may quibble about whether God existed prior to the Big Bang, but in terms of the language of physics, the question is meaningless. For when we say that *our* universe began at the Big Bang, we do not merely mean that the stuff (stars, comets, hydrogen atoms, etc.) came into being at that event, but that time and space and the laws of physics—which govern how reality is put together—also came into being at that instant. In light of this, it makes no sense for me to think about God existing in any meaningful way prior to the coming-into-existence of all of this. I am comfortable with the idea that God came into existence, as the complex system of laws and forces that define our universe, with (or as) the Big Bang. Some thinkers, physicists among them, believe that ours is only one in a string of universes. There may have been other universes that came into being, had long lives, and ceased to exist before ours. There are also those who postulate the existence of parallel universes that exist alongside ours. But we can have no knowledge of any of those other possible universes, since no signals can ever pass from one to another. So for all practical purposes our universe is sealed off from any other. The only meaningful context in which God might exist and function is that of our universe, which is *not* eternal but had its beginning at a specific point in the past.

When I first introduced the idea of God's consciousness being the emergent result of the interaction of all other consciousnesses, I rejected the notion that God is unchanging. I suggested that at some point in the distant past (perhaps with, or shortly after, the evolution of the neuron) God went from being nonconscious to being conscious, just as an embryo goes from being nonconscious (in the weeks before its first neurons form) to being conscious (at some later point; the exact point can be argued but it certainly cannot predate the formation of neurons). So just as God is not eternal, God is not unchanging. God develops.

The last, and perhaps most important, traditional assumption—namely, that God is absolutely superlative—presents a problem. I previously referred to *The Emergence of Everything*, in which Harold Morowitz sketches out 28 emergences that brought the universe from the Big Bang to our current state of consciousness, spirituality, and culture. Fascinating though it is, it left me wondering: Is that twenty-eighth emergence the end of the story? Has a 14-billion-year process culminated in the appearance of a thinking, believing, conscious human being? Logic suggests that the answer must be no. A process like emergence is, by definition, an ongoing one. Like evolution, each new emergence will—in the course of time—give rise to a newer and higher level of emergence. The fact that we cannot easily imagine what the next new emergence will be does not change the fact that it will happen. Carl Sagan noted that it was the height of arrogance and hubris (not to mention completely illogical) to assume that we are the only intelligent life form in the universe. The fact that we have not encountered other intelligent life forms (and may never encounter them) does not change the simple logic that sets the probability near zero of our earth's being absolutely unique in its ability to produce and sustain intelligent life.[28] I would argue similarly that the fact that we cannot imagine anything beyond the emergent state of divine consciousness does not mean that a next emergence will not occur. It is highly unlikely that it will occur soon enough for us to be aware of it, but our nonawareness or inability to imagine does not alter the probability that a new level *will* emerge.

As Sagan says, it would be the height of hubris and arrogance to suppose that our current state is the ultimate, final one. Our state is certainly ultimate and final for us, but not for the universe. This realization requires us to adopt a posture of tremendous humility. Neither the Earth, nor human beings, nor our technology is the crown of creation. Rather, we are all just another link in a chain stretching back in one direction to the beginning and in the other direction into some unknown and unfathomable future. In a fairly recent (in cosmic terms) link in that chain, a particular level of quantity, complexity, and interconnectedness was achieved by the neurons in our brains to produce an emergent level that we now call human consciousness. Once there were enough consciousnesses interconnecting with each other in a sufficiently complex manner, a new level of emergence occurred that I have identified as God's consciousness. The pattern that characterizes emergence now leads me to suggest with some confidence, albeit with absolutely no idea of the details, that something will emerge beyond what we currently identify as God.

I do not think that my rejection of the bedrock Jewish belief in God's eternity, God's unchangingness, and God's absoluteness undermines belief in general or belief in God in particular. The fact that the universe is not infinite in size does not make it any less awesome and wondrous. Similarly, the fact that God is not eternal, unchanging, or absolute does not make God any less worthy of reverence, awe, and perhaps even worship and obedience. The fact is that our own experience of awareness or consciousness is one of the most awesome and mysterious phenomena that we know of, so the existence of an even higher order of consciousness that exists as a result of the interconnectedness of all our human consciousnesses must take our breath away and inspire us to say, with the Psalmist, "Great is Adonai and most worthy of praise; there can be no measurement of God's greatness!"[29]

MOVING AHEAD

In this chapter I have laid out, in what I hope is a clear and convincing manner, how we might understand God as a sentient, conscious self, without taking a leap of faith into the realm of the supernatural. These views allow us to remain rooted in logic and rationality, yet still believe in the existence of God as an actual Presence. This is not a cleverly disguised humanism, but a rethinking of how we can fit traditional beliefs into a modern conceptual framework of a universe that is not magical but that operates according to inviolable rules of nature. We turn next to the question of how the idea of an emergent, conscious God might fit with one of the most ancient and fundamental Jewish notions—namely, the idea of mitzvah, or "commandment."

NOTES

1. Ps. 104:24.
2. I cannot imagine that this planet is the only one that has ever seen the development of life. The odds against our uniqueness are simply too great. For a compelling argument on this issue, see Carl Sagan, *The Varieties of Scientific Experience* (New York: Penguin Press, 2006), especially chapters 3 and 4.
3. Obviously these observations are based on our (still very incomplete) knowledge of the history of the Earth. If there are indeed life forms, and even conscious ones, elsewhere in the universe, then the time scales of this observation might prove inaccurate. For example, it may be that conscious life forms developed somewhere else in the universe while our solar system was still a whirling disk of dust and rocks, several billion years ago. The sequence that I am proposing, however, would still be present, even if the dates were to change by a billion or so years here or there.
4. Because the question of whether other conscious beings exist in the universe is an open and currently unresolvable one, I will continue to refer only to humans. But let us understand that what I am saying about God's consciousness includes all conscious beings, wherever they might exist in the universe.
5. The questions of whether the laws of physics existed before the Big Bang, or for that matter whether those laws exist in other universes—if there are other universes—fascinating as they may be, are unresolvable by contemporary physics.
6. The classical system of *Kabbalah*, or Jewish mysticism, did see God's absolute essence, which it labels *Ein Sof* (literally "without end" or "without boundary") as being utterly apart from the world and humanity, but then had to develop the system of Sefirot, or emanations, to allow for some sort of divine interaction with the world.
7. Babylonian Talmud, Sanhedrin 106b.
8. In the last century, the notion of God as changeable became one of the pillars of process theology, a branch, primarily, of Christian theology. For a treatment of the relationship between modern Jewish thought and process theology, see William E. Kaufman, *The Evolving God in Jewish Process Theology* (Lewiston, NY: Edwin Mellen Press, 1997).
9. Jerusalem Talmud, Hagigah 1:8 (76d), Jerusalem Talmud, Peah 2:6 (17a), and elsewhere.
10. In Hebrew the present tense of the verb "to be" is understood, not stated, so the simple pronoun "I" actually means "I am" if it is not accompanied by another verb.
11. Emil L. Fackenheim, *Quest for Past and Future: Essays in Jewish Theology* (Bloomington, IN: Indiana University Press, 1968), 146.
12. Babylonian Talmud, Menachot 29b.
13. The traditional style of lettering used by scribes in writing a Torah scroll requires that these flourishes be attached to the tops of seven Hebrew letters each time they appear.
14. Deut. 13:1.
15. Babylonian Talmud, Bava Metzia 59a–b.
16. Ex. 20:16.
17. *Mekhilta of Rabbi Ishmael, Bahodesh 11*, a relatively early (perhaps third or fourth century CE) compilation of midrash on the book of Exodus.
18. I am referring to the Second Temple, completed around 500 BCE, after the destruction of the First Temple by the Babylonians in 586 BCE. The First Temple, built by King Solomon, had itself been in existence for roughly three centuries.
19. It should be noted that although the traditional form of the requirement is that there be ten adult males, in our era the Reform, Reconstructionist, and (most) Conservative commu-

nities have discarded the gender element from the definition, but have maintained the core idea that the *minyan* is necessary.

20. The Hebrew word used in the sources is *shoteh*. It connotes insanity, cognitive limitation, or some other severe mental deficiency, although most dictionary renditions sound cruel and inhumane to contemporary readers living in a culture of maximal inclusion.

21. But note that the sources disqualify from the minyan only one who is both deaf and dumb: "But if he speaks but does not hear, or hears but does not speak, the rule for him is like that of a hearing person in all respects" (*Arukh Hashulchan*, Laws of Morning Blessings, 55:12).

22. Babylonian Talmud, Berakhot 58b.
23. Josh. 10:12–13.
24. Job 38:4, 12, 22.
25. Gen. 32:30.
26. Ex. 33:20.
27. Gen. 18:25.
28. See Sagan, *The Varieties of Scientific Experience*, chap. 4.
29. Ps. 145:3.

Chapter Four

Emergent God and Mitzvot/Commandments

The question before us is how the idea of God's emergent self, as described in the previous chapter, might affect our ideas about mitzvot (commandments) or halakha (Jewish law). Before we address the issue, however, it is important to understand the basics of the notions of law in general and Jewish law in particular.

LIVING WITH RULES

If I lived by myself, in complete isolation from all other human beings, I could do whatever I chose. But this is not the case. We human beings live in complex social networks from the moment we are born to the moment we die, and this means that we cannot do whatever we choose, but must limit our behaviors in countless ways to accommodate the constant presence of others. Thus religious traditions of all sorts, and societies in general, prescribe rules for human conduct and often include instructions about how society should respond when these rules are violated. The rules themselves lead to fascinating discussions.

Let's look at a simple example: The rule says one should not kill another person. It seems like a pretty simple rule. But does this rule mean you shouldn't kill anybody? Ever? Well, not quite. If someone tries to kill you and you have no other choice, it's not so terrible—according to the standards of most societies—if you kill your attacker first. And then, of course, there's the case of war, where you are not only allowed but commanded to kill the enemy. And then there's capital punishment—if Person A kills Person B, then many societies throughout the course of human history have held that the society (or occasionally the family of the victim) should kill Person A. But actually that gets even more complicated because capital punishment is sometimes deemed appropriate for crimes other than murder, cases that are *tantamount* to murder. Like (depending on your society) kidnapping. Or blaspheming. Or entering a sacred place where members of your caste don't belong. Actually, when we think about it, there are lots of exceptions to the rule about not killing people. It turns out not to be so simple after all.

The complexity of such discussions leads to a more fundamental question—namely, why are we supposed to obey the rules? What's the source of their authority? These questions begin to interest us in childhood. Early on, Mommy and Daddy make rules, and we, as very young children, must follow them because Mommy and Daddy are Mommy and Daddy. Their job is to tell us what to do. They also love us and feed us and take care of everything we need. In essence, they own us. That seems to give them the power, the right, and perhaps the responsibility to make whatever rules they wish. When we grow up a little and get out into the world, a surprise greets us: apparently, not everyone's Mommy and Daddy have the same rules as my Mommy and Daddy. At some friends' houses, they're allowed to eat sugary cereal for breakfast. And some kids can eat dinner in front of the television. Others have to address their Mommy and Daddy as "ma'am" and "sir" or take out the garbage every evening. We begin to see that rules are not universal, that they are often context-bound. In adulthood the state becomes a bit like our parents and makes and enforces its own rules. They are still context bound but the context is much more inclusive and broad. We know that certain behaviors that are permitted in our society are prohibited in others, but unless we move to the other societies, the difference doesn't matter very much.

In all these cases, the source of the rules is pretty clear. Whether I am happy with Mommy and Daddy's rules or not, it's clear that they *are* Mommy and Daddy's rules and that they *do* apply to me. I know that because when I am not under Mommy and Daddy's direct control—as for example, when I am out with friends (and Mommy and Daddy can't see me) or in school—the rules have less control over me. Likewise, I may or may not like the state's rules, but it is clear where they come from and by whom they are enforced. Whether the process is democratic or dictatorial, benevolent or malevolent, the system makes a certain kind of sense.

Finally, it is assumed in general that the person who makes the law has the right to change, amend, or abrogate it, but that those for whom the law is made and whose behavior it regulates have less power to do so. Thus if Mommy and Daddy say, "No television on school nights," *they* may occasionally decide to relax, change, or suspend the rule for some reason, but *I* have little if any power to change that rule.

LIVING WITH JEWISH RULES

How do these observations about rules in general apply to Jewish law? Sociologists might say that Judaism, like most other religions, makes rules in order to regulate the society constituted by its adherents. That would make it a lot like any other state. But that is not what the ancient sources of Judaism claim. Rather, they make a far more audacious claim about the rules—namely, that they are universal (not context-bound) rules laid down by a universal (not context-bound) supernatural, omnipotent God. This God is very clear that His[1] authority is exclusive and absolute. Here is just a small sample of the statements the Torah attributes to Him:

> I am The Eternal your God who brought you out of the land of Egypt, the house of bondage. You shall have no other gods beside Me.[2]
> You shall keep all My statutes and all My laws and do them: I am The Eternal.[3]
> Take care to do everything that I command you. Do not add to it or take away from it.[4]

These terse proclamations of authority are supported by numerous divine assurances that obedience to God's laws will result in great rewards—security, prosperity, fertility, and long life are chief among them—while disobedience will bring harsh punishment of all kinds. The laws and statutes referred to cover a very wide range of human behavior. Criminal law, civil law, national governance and military law, religious ritual law, and numerous types of regulations of personal behavior (e.g., eating, dress, sexual conduct, parent-child interactions, and so on) are included. The traditional rabbinic count of these biblical laws puts their number at 613.

Yet even with all these laws, the Bible leaves open many questions of how we are to behave. For example, regarding the Sabbath, the Torah tells us that we may not work, light fire, or leave our dwelling place. If one violates any of these prohibitions, capital punishment is prescribed. But the Torah does not specify what exactly constitutes work, or what it means to "light" fire, or how "dwelling places" are defined. Is playing music for pleasure considered work? What about gardening for pleasure? If a fire is burning before the Sabbath, may I continue to use its light and heat once the Sabbath begins? If so, may I add fuel to it? Do I have to stay in my house on the Sabbath? In my yard? In town? There are endless questions left unanswered by the Torah.

These questions are addressed in a body of work known collectively as the Oral Law, a very large corpus of interpretive legal discussions and pronouncements that come down to us in the Mishnah, the Gemara,[5] a number of legal midrashic (expository) works, and a wide variety of law codes and commentaries composed starting in the Middle Ages and continuing until today. In these collections the details of how to live our lives are worked out in what appear to be logical legal arguments among legal scholars. In other words, it would *seem* that the actual details of the laws are the result of human interpretation, although the underlying principles come with a claim of divine authorship. The claim is that God handed down the basic principles, but human beings are responsible for deciding how those principles should be translated into clear rules for everyday life. But at least one strand of the tradition itself denies that this is so. Instead it claims that God revealed the law to Moses from the very beginning of the process in two forms, one written and one oral. One midrash describes Moses's actions while receiving the Torah on Mount Sinai for forty days thus: "He studied the written law by day, and the oral law by night."[6] And probably the most famous and comprehensive statement of this notion comes from Maimonides's own introduction to his 14-volume legal code, the *Mishneh Torah*. There he describes how Moses received the Torah on Mount Sinai:

> All the mitzvot that were given to Moses at Sinai were given with their explanations, as it is written, "I will give you the tablets of stone, with the Torah, and the mitzvah" (Ex. 24:12). "Torah" means the Written Torah, while "the mitzvah" means its explanation. And God commanded us to observe the Torah according to the mitzvah. And "the mitzvah" is what is called the Oral Torah. Moses wrote the whole Torah before his death in his own hand, gave a copy to every tribe and placed one copy in the Ark for all time . . . . And the mitzvah, which is the explanation of the Torah, he did not write, but rather commanded it orally to the Elders, to Joshua, and to all Israel. . . . This is why it is called "Oral Torah." Now even though the Oral Torah was not written, Moses taught it in his academy to all 70 Elders of Israel. And Elazar, Pinchas and Joshua, all three received it from Moses. And to Joshua, who was the disciple of Moses our Teacher, he passed on the Oral Torah and commanded him regarding it. Similarly, Joshua taught orally all his life. Many Elders received it from Joshua, and Eli received it from the Elders and from Pinchas. Samuel received it from Eli and his academy; David received it from Samuel and his academy.[7]

As he goes on, Maimonides lays out the chain of tradition all the way to his own day. So this entire strand of tradition claims that even the Oral Law, which appears to be wholly the product of human discussion and interpretation, is in fact a part of direct divine revelation.

If one does not accept this claim entirely, but rather espouses the still rather traditional view that God lays down the basic principles of the Torah while rabbis hammer out the details, then a whole cluster of questions comes up. Which rabbis are empowered to decide on the details? Can any individual decide on the details for himself or herself? Should a local community vote on the details? Or should the local community perhaps be responsible for choosing one or more rabbis who will decide on the details? Once the rules have been laid out, who may change them? Under what conditions? And, perhaps most important, what is the relationship between the divinely revealed principles and the humanly agreed-upon details?

To many contemporary Jews, these issues seem unimportant, a waste of time as silly as arguing about how many angels can dance on the head of a pin. But to me they are crucial to understanding what Jewish life is all about. There is no question that Jewish life, in its more traditional forms, involves a large number of mitzvot, "commandments" that one is supposed to observe. We are supposed to keep kosher, observe the Sabbath, circumcise our sons, refrain from eating any leavened food during Passover, sit *shiva*—that is, observe very specific mourning practices for seven days—for our dead, pray three times a day, study Torah, recite blessings over many daily activities (including eating, using the bathroom, putting on new clothes, seeing the ocean, and more; one tradition recommends no fewer than one hundred blessings every day), give *tzedakah* (literally "righteousness," but in reality the mitzvah of giving to the poor), and many, many others. The list seems endless, and we often judge how religious a Jew is (actually, "how observant" is a better term, but the distinction is usually ignored) by how many of these mitzvot he or she performs. Further, we often casually define the three major[8] movements of American Judaism by the quantity of mitzvot their adherents allegedly observe: the Orthodox do them all, the Conservative do many, and the Reform do only a few. (In reality this is a misleading and not very useful stereotype of these movements, but it is certainly the way they are most commonly perceived.) In fact, I would argue that one of the key things that makes Jewish life Jewish is the religious behaviors it entails. Of course Jewish theology is special and Jewish ethics/values are lovely, but frankly I am not convinced that these aspects of Jewish life are unique. Rather, Jewish uniqueness lies in how Jews live, and that has traditionally been a function of mitzvot (i.e., divinely revealed principles) and halakha (i.e., the details of the laws, as worked out, one way or another, by human beings).

The question is, why bother? Why do we do all these things, especially since they make life somewhat more complicated? It is apparently a rather difficult question for modern Jews, if we may judge by the very large number of modern Jews who have chosen *not* to do these things.

THE ANATEVKA ANSWER

There are a few basic answers to the question. An ancient response was that we should continue to observe the laws because failure to do so will result in divine punishment. This approach fell into disfavor fairly early, however, as we observed many nonobservant Jews not being struck by lightning, plague, or other divine chastisements. A second response was to insist that even if

God would not rain obvious punishment down on the heads of the nonobservant, the laws were still God's laws and that fact alone ought to be enough to compel obedience. Without sanctions, however, this approach appealed only to the most pious or the most theologically inspired—which is to say, to a small minority of Jews. A much more common answer is expressed by Tevye in the opening moments of the classic Broadway musical *Fiddler on the Roof*, when he describes all the traditions that characterize life in his small *shtetl*. "Here in Anatevka, we have traditions for everything—how to eat, how to sleep, how to wear clothes. For instance, we always keep our heads covered, and always wear a little prayer shawl. This shows our constant devotion to God. You may ask, how did this tradition get started? I'll tell you. I don't know. But it's a tradition."[9]

This answer, which is not really an answer at all, was sufficient for many Jews during many centuries of premodern Jewish life. We do things the way we do them because that's the way we've always done them. It's who we are and we don't really think too much about why. This answer worked as long as Jews in the premodern world had little choice about how to live their lives. Their world afforded them little or no mobility. There was a high probability that one would live one's entire life and die in more or less the same circumstances—the same geographical area, the same socioeconomic class, the same religious lifestyle, the same level of education—as one's parents, grandparents, and great-grandparents. Social change moved at a glacial pace. The maintenance of Jewish tradition was enforced both from within and from without. It was enforced from without because, especially in premodern Christian Europe, the larger community placed restrictions on Jewish life that limited where and how Jews could live.

This ghettoized situation, which we moderns tend to think of in solely negative terms as discrimination, had a silver lining in that it gave the Jewish community a fair amount of autonomous jurisdiction over its members and their lives. What happened within the ghetto walls was, for the most part, controlled by those who lived there. Public behavior was fairly well regulated (although private behavior was always harder to control). The community could fine its members or garnish their wages, and social and economic ostracism were widely used to enforce standards of behavior. The community even used corporal punishment (flogging), though it is not clear how often this measure was employed. In these circumstances there was little reason for most Jews to wonder why they ought to live as they did. It was, as Tevye tells us, a tradition.

This all changed with the dawn of modernity when Enlightenment and Emancipation slowly gave Jews rights to live where and how they chose. The same processes also stripped the Jewish community of its power to enforce its own rules. Over a period of no more than two hundred years, from the late eighteenth to the late twentieth century, Jews went from a position of having little choice about how to live to having almost unlimited choice. Now, as we are well aware, Jews are free to dress, eat, work, marry, and conduct their religious lives (or not) as they see fit. Such freedom inevitably leads back to the question: why, especially at this point in our history, should we follow the mitzvot laid down by tradition?

Once the conditions of modernity make the question inevitable and unavoidable, it seems that there are a limited number of possible answers. One, of course, is that there is no reason whatsoever to follow the mitzvot. This is clearly a response favored by many contemporary Jews. In a society in which religious observance is a matter of voluntary compliance, and where there are few if any negative consequences attached to nonobservance, many Jews choose not to follow the dictates of their tradition. For the better part of a century, American Jews have abandoned many of the ritual behaviors that once characterized Jewish life. This has led to an endless variety of redefinitions of the "essence" of Judaism, including arguments that Jewish life at its core is about ethical monotheism, prophetic/social justice, ethical humanism, and more. I do not want to address or analyze these options here. Suffice it to say that over the course of my life, I have personally come to value highly a life of Jewish observance—and so I am more interested in exploring possible reasons for observance, rather than the reasons put forward for the abandonment of mitzvot.

MY PATH TO OBSERVANCE

This statement deserves some explanation. I am not claiming that I have come to deep and meaningful insights about Judaism, God, and mitzvot, and that therefore I live a fairly traditional Jewish life. Reasonable as that might seem, it is not the sequence of steps that I have experienced, nor is it a sequence experienced by many individuals whose lifestyles include a significant amount of religious observance. Instead things often seem to go the other way around, with some sort of attraction to traditional observance coming first and then leading to a search for reasons to justify it. My own case may provide a useful example.

I grew up in a fairly nonobservant social context. My parents instilled in me a strong sense of Jewish identity—that is, pride in asserting quite consciously that I am a Jew—but my identity was not framed by much in the way of religious observance. We lit Hannukah candles, had a seder at Passover, and were quite involved in synagogue life, but that was about the extent of it. My parents had been born into very traditional Eastern European immigrant homes— both were the first generation in their families to be born in the United States—so they knew the traditions. They had left those traditions behind, as did a very large proportion of their generation, in the process of becoming American. They went to college, became professionals, moved to the suburbs, and succeeded quite well in fitting into the American scene of their time. They were essentially drawing a distinction between Jewish identity and Jewish observance. Jewish identity was strong in my family but observance of mitzvot was all but nonexistent.

My "rebellion" began in high school and evolved for the next decade or so. A few of the landmarks in that rebellious development were my decision to start wearing a *kippah* (*yarmulke* or skullcap) on the Sabbath, my excitement at studying Torah under the tutelage of a few charismatic young rabbinical students from Hebrew Union College–Jewish Institute of Religion, my decision to keep kosher in my apartment and, a year later, to observe these dietary restrictions outside the apartment as well, my decision to wear my kippah all the time (instead of just on the Sabbath), and my purchase of—and decision to use daily—a *tallit* and *tefillin*. Early in this process I decided to become a rabbi. Most of these decisions were made on a gut level. They were not the result of a carefully reasoned thought process. Some were inspired by charismatic teachers whom I was drawn to imitate. Others resulted from a desire to be different, to craft an identity that was uniquely mine. And still others resulted from the cultural forces of the late 1960s and early 1970s, when ethnic identity was trendy and popular and when being Jewishly observant was "cool." But there was neither any logical analysis nor any grand "Ah ha!" moment of revelation or insight that led me to modify how I lived. Rather, the lifestyle gradually grew on me and felt right. The thinking through of *why* these things are important came after the fact. Having adopted various Jewish practices, I felt the need to understand why these behaviors were important and meaningful to me. My intellectual curiosity would not allow me to feel satisfied with Tevye's answer.

Once the need for analysis and understanding became apparent, it seemed clear where I would end up. I could not accept the traditional explanation— that is, that an eternal, omnipotent, sentient God, who had created the universe and chosen to enter into a covenant with the people of Israel, had revealed these laws to Moses on Sinai. This was not an option for two reasons. First of all, I did not and do not believe these things about God, as I have already explained. And second, even if I had been able to accept the view of God as an omniscient, aware Being, I could not imagine why the One who was responsible for creating and maintaining the entire universe over the course of its 14 billion years could possibly care about whether I moved my neighbor's property line marker or whether I recited Sh'ma Yisrael ("Hear O Israel") at the proper time of day. These are local, parochial concerns that could not possibly interest or occupy the *Ribono Shel Olam*, the "Master of the Universe." To believe otherwise would require a completely unreasonable and enormously arrogant sense of the uniqueness and importance of our planet, the role of humans on it, and the role of the Jewish people among all humans. The more I learned about the vastness of the cosmos, the less appealing such beliefs became. They are the height of hubris. I have always preferred a more humble view of the role of humans in the grand cosmic scheme.

If the traditional explanation was not an option, what was left to explain my passion for Shabbat observances, my love of Torah study, and my decision to keep kosher? There are two main possibilities. The first is the idea that the ancient laws of Judaism somehow encode very deep and cherished values. They are meant to teach us important lessons. So, for example, Shabbat observance is meant to teach us the value of slowing down, taking time on a regular basis to "smell the flowers," and avoiding the trap of coming to worship our work, our creativity, and the benefits they bring us. Keeping kosher is meant to teach us to be aware of what and how we eat—that is, to eat mindfully—and perhaps to warn us against cruelty, for what could be more cruel than cooking meat (a foodstuff that can only be acquired by bringing death to an animal) in milk, a food that by its nature symbolizes mother-love and its life-giving power?

This system of understanding mitzvot has some great advantages. It is wholly rational and demands no theological leaps of faith. It aims to convince us of the value and purpose of the mitzvot. But it also has two major disadvantages. The first is that it deals with each behavioral requirement separately, never addressing or recognizing an entire system of mitzvot. This means that every single candidate for mitzvah-status must be judged on its own terms, and this can lead to a strange assortment of individual patchwork versions of Jewish life, with each individual adopting behaviors that seem meaningful to him or her. Such a situation makes the creation of community difficult, for communities are identified in large part by shared practices. The second disadvantage is that mitzvot that do not seem to encode a valuable lesson have no chance of surviving. Thus, while sitting in a *sukkah* may teach about the fragility of life, waving the *lulav* (a bouquet of palm, willow, and myrtle branches) and *etrog* (citron) seem to teach nothing at all and might therefore be abandoned as meaningless. Such a sifting method, I think, leads to the significant impoverishment of Jewish tradition in the long run.

There is a second possible approach to mitzvot that avoids both the objectionable assumptions related to a supernatural, sentient Creator–Legislator and the impoverishment that can come from a values-based evaluation approach. It comes in the thought of Rabbi Mordecai Kaplan, the twentieth century founder of Reconstructionist Judaism. The title of Rabbi Kaplan's seminal work, *Judaism as a Civilization*, says it all. We are, he claimed, a civilization, a People, and we function in ways that are similar to the ways that any other civilization functions. One of the things that civilizations do is develop what may be called folkways or customs. These are behaviors that are characteristic of the civilization (although they may be shared by other civilizations) and that help to create a sense of community and belonging among the members of the group. So, for example, most Americans eat turkey on Thanksgiving. Often even people who don't enjoy turkey, and don't eat it during the year, eat it on Thanksgiving. It is remarkable to see how many expatriate Americans get together to eat turkey on Thanksgiving in Paris, Madrid, London, Tokyo, and Jerusalem. It is one of the ways that they maintain their connection with home, even after years of living outside of the United States. It is, if you like, one of the mitzvot associated with being American.

Of course such customs do more than simply create cohesion among those who practice them, though that is their primary purpose. They symbolize and express the values of the civilization of which they are a part. So although there is nothing inherently symbolic about turkey, the message of Thanksgiving—as we were taught it in elementary school—is clear: our ancestors came to a new land seeking freedom and barely survived the harsh conditions of this new place. They were aided in their survival by friendly Native Americans who taught them how to grow corn and hunt wild turkeys. In gratitude for their survival and their newfound friends, the pilgrims celebrated the first Thanksgiving. That's the story I learned as a boy. It is not very important that the story be historically accurate. What's important is that the story be a compelling part of the collective memory of the people who tell it, not that it reflect precisely what happened. Historians of the period tell us that the story I learned in grade school is not terribly close to the way things actually went for the Puritan pilgrims of Plymouth colony. The discrepancies are important for historians, but not for Americans. Memory is what counts, not history. Our childhood Thanksgiving lessons, and the customs that go with them (turkey, cranberries, sweet potatoes, and pumpkin pie), are lessons about being American. Friendship with neighbors and gratitude for the bounty that is ours are important pillars of our society.

All civilizations build a sense of belonging by developing concrete behavioral customs, and that is how Kaplan's system regarded mitzvot. Shabbat observance was no more commanded by the omnipotent Creator of Heaven and Earth than cranberry relish, but it was one of the ways that Jewish civilization encoded values of the sanctity of time and the essential equality of all individuals (since on Shabbat even servants and employees get a day off). The observances of Passover teach us about the blessings of freedom and the evils of slavery. And the regular, halakhically prescribed giving of tzedakah (charity) teaches that all of us are responsible for improving the world. It is not hard to see how these customs, the Jewish equivalents of grade school Thanksgiving lessons, are taught to Jewish children to make them feel part of Jewish civilization as well as imparting to them Jewish values. Taken together with a large number of other customs—that is to say, mitzvot—they provide a sense of belonging to a Jewish Peoplehood, they distinguish Jews from those who are not part of their civilization, and they provide the Jewish people with constant reminders of their civilization's basic values.

I believe that most contemporary American Jews who observe Jewish tradition at all, and who think about it at all, do so in this "Kaplanian" fashion, whether or not they have ever heard of Kaplan or Reconstructionism. It is a reasonable approach to things. It regards behaviors as symbols—that is, as signposts pointing toward deeper meanings. And it identifies these values specifically as belonging to a community, a Jewish Peoplehood. It makes us feel a part of that Peoplehood. It is *not* very theological. All in all, it is a very compelling model.

WHEN CIVILIZATION ISN'T ENOUGH

Even though Kaplan's understanding of mitzvot as the customs of Jewish civilization seems altogether reasonable to contemporary Jews, it was quite a revolutionary challenge to an important element of Jewish tradition. For centuries, although most Jews would not have objected to the notion that mitzvot were the distinguishing customs of Jewish Peoplehood, they would not have accepted that as the primary understanding of the mitzvah system. Rather, the tradition—starting in the Torah and going forward—is quite clear: Mitzvot are the expression of our relationship with God, our covenant. God chose Abraham, and as part of the covenant God instructed him to circumcise himself and his sons. God freed us from Egyptian slavery and instructed us to remember the event and the relationship it symbolized by observing Passover. God created the world in six days and rested on the seventh day, and therefore commanded us to work for six days and rest on the seventh. The fact that these mitzvot end up being the customs that distinguish us as a civilization is a worthwhile fringe benefit, but it is hardly the main reason for observing God's mitzvot or the halakha that translates them into a set of rules regulating daily behavior. These rules are part and parcel of the mutual agreement between God and the People of Israel. In that relationship, according to the Torah's description, each party does something important for the other. God's obligation is to be Israel's God, protect us, and ensure our welfare; our job is to obey God.

It is important to understand the real impact of the formulation of mitzvot-as-relationship-with-God. Whatever other benefits may accrue to us from our Jewish observances, the *real* purpose of those behaviors—according to this traditional view—is to express our sense of connection with and relationship to God. We do these Jewish things because God commanded them. By way of analogy, imagine that you meet and fall in love with an individual who loves opera, and imagine further that you have never had any exposure to opera at all. Your new lover makes it clear that if you really love him or her it is very important that you accompany him or her to the opera on a regular basis. And because your love is deep and wonderful, you agree. It means so much to your lover. He or she simply glows with pleasure when you go along to the opera. It is the only demand the relationship really makes on you. Now over the course of time, you become quite comfortable with the routine of the opera. You come to enjoy getting dressed up, you admire the lovely décor in the opera house, and the music itself even grows on you. You meet friends whose opera subscription puts them in the seats right behind you every week. You learn a little Italian, which you've always wanted to do. In fact, opera becomes part of the way you define yourself. You actually come to enjoy the whole thing. But in the final analysis, you go to the opera as a way of expressing your love for your beloved.

This scenario suggests that relationships are sometimes so important to us that their very existence has a commanding power. The extent of the power may vary. So if I generally enjoy opera, but tonight I find myself too tired or too busy and thus would rather not go, my beloved's plea that I attend may be just enough to convince me. In a variant of the scenario, one could imagine an individual who, despite years of trying, just never warms up to opera—hates it, in fact. Nevertheless, this person so cares for his or her significant other that she or he goes to the opera anyway, at least occasionally, *solely* because the lover wishes it.[10] In either case the point is that sometimes the primary reason for our behavior is simply to express our caring for another.

If we turn now from opera to Judaism, we see that one way to think of the religious behavior prescribed in the Torah—or more broadly of the behavior prescribed by Jewish tradition in general—is as a sign of relationship with God. This shift in thinking adds a whole new level to the meaning of mitzvah, taking it way beyond the notion of behavior as encoded message about values, or custom as marker of group identity. Rather, this new level sees mitzvot as expressions of relationship with God. According to this view, putting up a *mezuzah* on the doorframe of my house is more than just a symbolic way of expressing the sanctity of "home," and more than just a way of marking my home as a Jewish home (though it is also both of these). Now it is also a way of expressing my relationship with God. The system of mitzvot can thus be seen as a system of spiritual practice and covenantal behavior. I find this understanding to be a source of great richness in life. The simplest act of religious life is no longer just a symbolic behavior that communicates values, and no longer just a way of identifying with my ethnic group. It is now a moment of spiritual reflection, a reminder of profound relationship.

But now we've circled back to our starting point. I *don't* believe that the Creator of Heaven and Earth is a sentient being who, long before the first instant of Creation, had mapped out the plans by which the Jewish people should live, even though this claim is axiomatic for much of the tradition, as we see in this lovely midrash:

> "In the beginning God created . . . ." (Gen. 1:1). Six things preceded the creation of the world. Among them are things that were created and things the creation of which was [merely] planned. The Torah and the Throne of Glory were created. . . Rabbi Huna and Rabbi Jeremiah said in the name of Rabbi Samuel son of Rabbi Isaac: The thought of [i.e., the plan to create] Israel preceded everything. A parable: A king was married to a fine lady, but he had no son from her. Once the king was passing through the market and said, "Take these pens and ink for my son." Everyone said, "He has no son, yet he says, 'Take these pens and ink for my son.'" People responded and said, "The king is a great seer. If the king had not foreseen that he would someday raise up a son from her, he would not have said, 'Take these pens and ink for my son.'" Similarly, if the Holy Blessed One had not foreseen that after twenty-six generations Israel would accept the Torah, He would not have written in the Torah, "Command the Israelites." "Speak to the Israelites."[11]

So according to this midrash, even before God created the universe, He wrote the Torah in anticipation of the eventual existence of the people of Israel and their willingness to accept it. This is a lovely idea. The problem is that it violates my belief in the nonsentient nature of the forces that brought the universe into being. So how can I claim that mitzvot are all about my relationship with God?

THE COMMANDING VOICE OF THE EMERGENT GOD

Mordecai Kaplan's view of Jewish law, and the view of many contemporary liberal Jews, sees human creativity and authorship in the Torah, its laws, and the entire halakhic system. The traditional view sees divine creativity and authorship in them. The problem is that most people see the argument between these two views as an either/or proposition: *either* the laws were given to us by God *or* they were formulated by our very own ancestors.

This distinction was clearly foremost in the minds of the rabbis of the Talmudic and Medieval periods as they discussed the differences between laws that are *D'oraita* (an Aramaic term, literally "from the Torah") and laws that are *D'rabbanan* (literally "from the rabbis"). A law that is deemed D'oraita is taken more seriously, and is less open to question, interpretation, and change than one that is D'rabbanan. The former category is seen as imposing a deeper and more fundamental level of obligation. So, for example, the obligation to recite *Kiddush*, the blessings of sanctification over wine, on Friday evening at the beginning of Shabbat, is—according to the rabbis—a D'oraita obligation for adult men. Women are obligated to recite

Kiddush as well, but the extension of the obligation to include them is only D'rabbanan. This particular case has practical ramifications. A man may say Kiddush on behalf of a woman, but according to traditional legal standards, a woman may not recite Kiddush on behalf of a man. This is because of a principle that says that person X may only fulfill a mitzvah on behalf of person Y if person X is under the same obligation at the same level or at a "higher" level than person Y. But if person X is obligated at a lower level, then he or she may not fulfill the mitzvah on behalf of person Y. Thus a man, obligated to recite Kiddush D'oraita, may fulfill the obligation on behalf of another man or on behalf of a woman; but a woman, obligated to recite it D'rabbanan, may not fulfill it on a man's behalf. Essentially, although the debates are sometimes quite intricate, the distinction boils down to whether any particular law was given by God in the Torah or legislated by human beings.

But by thinking of God's consciousness as the emergent result of the massively complicated interaction among all other (primarily human) consciousnesses, I am suggesting that this either/or dichotomy is false and that it presents us with a false choice. The laws—that is to say, the mitzvot and the halakha—are the product of human legislation *and therefore are of divine origin*. The entire process of initial human legislation, and subsequent study of and constant and ongoing revision of the law, can be seen as a divine process.

I want to be very clear here. This is not some sleight of hand, whereby I acknowledge that the laws are truly of human origin but claim that they are really divine, the way you sometimes find "Made in China" stickers on the back of souvenirs that claim to be "genuine" and "local" in gift shops from the Grand Canyon to the Florida Everglades to the rocky coast of Maine. Rather, I am arguing that the human legislative process, especially when it is a communal and interactive process, *is* a divine process. There is nothing more to God's mind, where the laws originate, than the interactions among vast numbers of human minds over the generations, just as there is nothing more to my mind than the vast numbers of neuronal interactions inside my brain. There is no way to distinguish between those mitzvot that are God's will and those that are only human because there *is no distinction between the two*.

I would suggest this as a creative interpretation of the Talmudic story of Aknai's oven, which I referenced briefly in the previous chapter.[12] The story begins with a disagreement over the ritual purity or impurity of an oven referred to as "Aknai's Oven" (the details of the issue are unimportant). Rabbi Eliezer held one view, while all his colleagues held the opposite view. In the course of the argument, Rabbi Eliezer adduced three miraculous proofs to bolster his position. After each miraculous demonstration, the other sages rejected the very notion of bringing miraculous events into legal decision making. Finally, Eliezer played his trump card: "If the law agrees with me, let it be proved in heaven." At that point a "heavenly voice" proclaimed, "Why do you disagree with Rabbi Eliezer? In all matters the law agrees with him!" Rabbi Joshua then replied to the heavenly voice by quoting a verse from the Torah, "It is not in heaven!"[13] Rabbi Joshua's retort is generally thought of as meaning that, although God gave the Torah originally, its interpretation had now passed over to the human domain and God's opinion no longer holds sway. But I see it differently. When Rabbi Joshua proclaims that "it is not in Heaven," what he means is that the Torah and the legal system are not the direct product of the same physical/cosmological forces that resulted in the structure of the heavens—stars, galaxies, planets, and so on—but are rather the product of God's consciousness, which is the emergent product of the interaction of human consciousnesses. It's not that God has no right to interfere in the rabbis' deliberations, but rather that such interference cannot come mysteriously from the "heavenly voice" of the cosmic Creator God; it may only come from the deliberative voice of the Legislator God, which is indistinguishable from the deliberative voice of human collective creativity and consciousness.

But what are we to make of the terms "Creator God" and "Legislator God"? Is this a dualistic system of two Gods? The answer is no. I am not proposing that the Creator God and the Legislator God are two different Gods. Rather, they are two parts—or stages—of the one God. The stage of God that is the complex of natural laws and forces that brought the universe from the Big Bang through roughly its first 13 billion years is what I am referring to as the Creator God. The stage that has become sentient in something less than the last billion years, as the emergent result of the evolution of sentience in the universe, is what I refer to as the Legislator God (but could also be thought of as the Covenant God, the God of pathos, and so on). They are no more different Gods than my 9-year-old self back in 1963 and my 60-year-old self in 2014 are different persons.

ARE ALL GOD'S COMMANDMENTS RIGHT?

Although God's Oneness is not a question, there are some serious challenges raised by what I am proposing. One is the question of how we know which commandments are right or good or moral and which are not. In the traditional system, there was a bedrock assumption that God is wholly just and wholly good, and therefore that anything demanded of us by such a supernatural God of Justice and Goodness would be just and good. That is to say, God was the standard for justice and goodness to which we human beings compared ourselves. The Psalmist's words are unequivocal:

> The Torah of The Eternal is pure, causing the soul to repent.
> The testimony of The Eternal is trustworthy, making the foolish wise.
> The orders of The Eternal are straight, causing the heart to rejoice.
> The mitzvah of The Eternal is clear, enlightening the eyes.
> The fear of The Eternal is pure, standing forever.
> The judgments of The Eternal are true, altogether righteous.[14]

But I am proposing a view of God that starts with human consciousness and thought, human creativity and decision making. God's consciousness emerges as a result of the interaction among all of us flawed, weak, imperfect human beings. Now it might make sense to assume that the laws promulgated by such a God would be somewhat more just and good than those decided on autocratically by a single individual. After all, one of the bases for democracy that makes it a better system than a dictatorship is that decisions made by a group usually—though not always—protect the group from the poor judgment of extreme or unbalanced or evil individuals. But there is no reason to assume that the laws of God, conceived of in this way, would be reliably or infallibly good and just. This conclusion makes religious life quite a bit more challenging than it was under the theological assumption that "just because God said so it must be right." Now I am faced with the difficult task of having to think about and evaluate commandments before blindly obeying them. I am responsible for my own behavior. It is not enough to pass that responsibility on to God and say, in effect, that I was only following orders and I am therefore not culpable. After World War II, the international legal and moral process determined that "I was just following orders" was not a valid defense of reprehensible action, and this conclusion must remain valid whether the orders were given by a military officer or by God.

This is not, however, a brand-new attitude toward God's word. In particular, two biblical narratives come to mind in which the individual's insistence on exercising personal moral judgment provides us with a model for our own behavior. The first exemplar is Abraham, who challenges God's resolve to utterly destroy the wicked cities of Sodom and Gomorrah. When God informs Abraham of the plan to devastate the two cities, Abraham responds:

> Will You sweep away the righteous along with the wicked? Perhaps there are fifty righteous within the city. Will You sweep [it] away and not forgive the place for the sake of the fifty righteous who are in its midst? Far be it from You to do such a thing, to kill righteous with wicked so that righteous and wicked are [treated] the same! Far be it from You! Will the Judge of all the earth not do justice?[15]

This gutsy outburst from Abraham is the start of a conversation in which he appears to convince God, by stages, not to destroy the city if there are found 50, or 45, or 40, or 30, or 20, or even 10 righteous individuals in it. In the end the destruction goes ahead, and the righteous—the eight members of Lot's immediate family—are evacuated before the catastrophe hits.

The story raises many questions, but the one aspect that is important for us here is Abraham's refusal to accept God's decree without challenging its rightness. A somewhat looser translation might render the phrase "Far be it from You" (*chalila l'kha*) as "Shame on you!" Abraham seems to have figured out that he has the right, perhaps even the responsibility, to exercise his own powers of moral judgment even on the decrees of God. (Before we laud Abraham as an early theological hero, however, we should note that for some unfathomable reason he chooses *not* to exercise these same powers of moral judgment when God commands him to sacrifice his son Isaac in chapter 22.) A similar approach appears during the story of the exodus from Egypt, this time with Moses as the protagonist. During the time that Moses has been with God receiving the Torah, the people have built and worshipped a golden calf. God is outraged at this flagrant rejection of the exclusive monotheism demanded in the Ten Commandments and says to Moses, "Now let Me be, that My anger may burn against them and consume them, and I will make *you* into a great nation."[16] Moses's response seems an echo of Abraham's:

> Why, O Eternal God, would Your anger burn against Your people whom You brought out of Egypt with great strength and a mighty hand? Why? The Egyptians will say, "With evil intent did he bring them out, to kill them in the mountains, and to finish them off from the face of the earth!" Turn back from Your burning anger and change Your mind regarding this evil toward Your people. Remember what You said to Abraham, to Isaac and to Jacob, Your servants to whom You swore by Yourself, "I will increase your offspring as the stars of the sky, and I will give this entire land of which I have spoken to your offspring and they shall inherit it forever."[17]

This is quite an extended and eloquent appeal from a man who had earlier complained to God that he was not the right one for the job of leading Israel out of Egypt because he was "slow of speech and slow of tongue."[18] Unlike Abraham's purely principled argument ("Will the Judge of all the earth not do justice?"), Moses bases his plea in politics and public relations ("What will the Egyptians say?"), as well as principle, but it is no less a reflection of his commitment to personal analysis and evaluation of the rightness (or wrongness) of God's decree.

The same theme, in a much more modern context, is found in a story told of Rabbi Levi Yitzchak of Berditchev (1740–1809):

> When Yom Kippur ended R. Levi Yitzhaq [of Berditchev] beckoned to a tailor and asked him to relate to the congregation the argument which he had had that day with the Master of the World.

The tailor began in a trembling voice:
"I told the Master of the World: 'Today is the Day of Judgment. One must repent. But I did not sin much. I took a little leftover cloth from the rich. . . . And once I drank a small glass of brandy in the house of the *Poretz* [Squire] and took a bite of bread without washing my hands. These are all my transgressions.

"'But You, Master of the World, how many are Your transgressions! Why have You taken away small children who had not sinned? And from others You have taken the mothers of such children! But, Master of the World, I shall forgive You Your transgressions and may You forgive me mine, and let us drink *L'Hayyim!* [To Life!].'"

And as he related all this, the tailor drank *L'Hayyim* to the Master of the World.

The rabbi said after Yom Kippur:
"The tailor with his arguments saved the Jews. But a tailor remains a tailor. In exchange for a little leftover cloth he forgave the Master of the World such great sins! I, in that hour, would have asked another thing—that He should send us His Messiah to redeem the Jews. . . ."[19]

Again, not only does this tradition permit the Jews to question whether God's decrees have been altogether right, but the implication is that doing so is our responsibility, our obligation.

In a well-known dialogue by Plato entitled *Euthyphro*, the Greek philosopher Socrates asks Euthyphro whether the pious is loved by the gods because it is pious, or is something pious because it is loved by the gods? The underlying question is whether God is the *source* of our sense of piety (or, by analogy, goodness, justice, etc.) or whether God responds positively to those things that have a goodness and righteousness independent of God's endorsing them. The examples of Abraham and Moses seem clearly to support the latter view, though there are numerous other biblical narratives that would call it into question. Abraham *knows* what justice looks like, and the destruction of the innocent together with the guilty does not meet the test.

This leaves open the question of *how* Abraham, or Moses, or any of us come to know right and wrong, good and evil, just and unjust. Are they somehow part of our biology, an adaptive trait granted us by the evolutionary process? Or are they a function of culture, with each society developing its own moral sense and teaching it to its children from their earliest years? These are hugely complex and probably unanswerable questions, but a few things seem clear:

- We *do* have a sense of right and wrong, good and evil.
- The distinctions in our minds between right and wrong are sometimes crystal clear and at other times fuzzy and uncertain.
- The divine teachings of theistic religious traditions are not necessarily the only, or the clearest, or the best source of such distinctions.

Unfortunately, it is also quite clear that human beings do not always act in accordance with what is generally agreed to be good, just, and righteous. Often they act counter to those standards, usually because they sense that there is an overriding principle at work—namely, that the behavior in question will lead to pleasure, or advantage, or comfort, or security for them, their family, or their nation. Such self-interest often overrides the evil that the action in question may bring to others.

If God's consciousness, God's mind, that part of God that cares about human behavior, is the emergent function of the hugely complex interaction of huge numbers of consciousnesses, it is clear that some of the judgments made by God might *not* be right or good, since some of the judgments made by human beings are not right or good. Sometimes God will command behavior that is just and good, and sometimes God will command behavior that is just plain wrong. At first blush this is a heretical and blasphemous claim. Yet there are several ways of thinking about the issue that may take the sting out of our initial discomfort with it.

First of all, many modern people have already accepted the idea that there is a wide variety of natural events that have tragic consequences for human beings. Since the 1981 publication of Harold Kushner's *When Bad Things Happen to Good People*, it has become less and less shocking to suggest—contrary to the conviction of ancient Jewish tradition—that deadly tumors or earthquakes are not "planned" or "sent" by a sentient, moral God who uses them as chastisements. Rather, such catastrophes are simply accidents, random consequences of the fact that nature is a highly complex system that we often cannot understand. A hurricane is not evil at all. It is simply nature's way of coping with the complex dynamics of air, water, temperature, and fluid flow on our planet. What is tragic is that human beings accidentally get in the way of a hurricane and lose their property, or their lives. The same may be said of blizzards, earthquakes, volcanoes, and so on. These events are part of nature. That they sometimes have tragic consequences for us is an accident, not a plan.

The problem arises when we conclude, based on this analysis, that such *natural* events can't be blamed on God, but that *human* events are different. If a town is wiped out by an earthquake, we must come to terms with the terrible tragedy but not be angry at God; but when a town is wiped out by religious fanatics who say that God told them to destroy it because its inhabitants were evil, or nonbelievers, or the wrong color, *then* we can be outraged. In such a case, we have a few different choices. One is to claim that God did *not* command the atrocity, because God is absolutely and always good and this was clearly an evil act, not a good one. The perpetrators *say* God commanded them but in reality they are fabricating this evil claim. It is they who are solely responsible for their cruelty, and they have only compounded the evil of the act by claiming it was a divine commandment. This analysis preserves God's absolute moral goodness while admitting that human beings are sometimes deeply flawed or downright evil. God and religion come out unscathed and we come to terms once more with the ancient truth that people can often behave in horrifying ways.

A second, very different analysis takes the perpetrators' claim at face value and concludes that God is in fact sometimes evil, and that therefore religion is evil and we would be better off, as a species, without it. This is a position taken more and more often in our world as the number of atrocities committed by religious fanatics of all stripes increases. A group of religious extremists commits an act of cruelty or murder and many people say, "If this be religion, and if that be God, I want nothing of it."

I would question both of these conclusions. Let's go back for a moment to the realm of natural disasters. Imagine a case where a good, kind, sweet person is afflicted by a terrible disease, suffers horribly for months, and finally dies. Theologically speaking, we can parse these awful events in a few different ways. One way is to rage at God for the terrible injustice, abandon all faith, and reject God, religion, and all it stands for. This is not an uncommon scenario. I know personally of several people who were driven away from all ties to religious life by such theological crises. Such a response amounts to saying "Any God who would do such a thing deserves no love or faith or obedience from me," and some people actually articulate their feelings in words very similar to these. Another reaction to natural tragedy, as suggested by Kushner and others, is to claim that such awful events are not God's fault at all. They are simply accidents of nature, independent of God. One can still have faith, believe in God, and be comforted by religion, although one might have to give up the traditional notion that God controls all things. Instead one would be left to conclude that God is good and kind and loving, and that God controls *some* things, but that this dreadful event was not controlled by God. This train of thought might lead to a further question of whether God does not control such events because God is unable to do so, or because God somehow chooses not to do so, but the result is the same: God's power has been taken down a peg, but otherwise God and religion survive.

However, Jewish tradition suggests a third, more challenging way to understand the event. We might insist on God's absolute power, reject all dualism (that is, the notion that the world consists of two sorts of events, those under God's control and those not under God's control), and live—if in perplexed discomfort—with our belief that God brings about both good and bad things. The prophet Isaiah quotes God as claiming to "fashion light and create darkness, make peace and create evil."[20] This line finds its way into the daily morning liturgy, in the first of the two blessings preceding Sh'ma Yisrael, in a somewhat modified, or "cleaned-up" form. We acknowledge God as the one who "fashions light and creates darkness, makes peace and creates everything." The minor change from "creates evil" to "creates everything" takes a bit of the sting out of this proclamation, but only a bit. A similar view is found in the Mishnah where we read, "One is required to recite a blessing over evil just as he recites a blessing over good."[21]

The point of both of these texts is that at least one strand of mainstream Jewish thought has preferred the view of God as controlling everything, including that which is tragic or painful, over the view that there are some things that are outside of God's control. Given the choice between a worldview that allows God to be completely good but denies God omnipotence (and therefore, perhaps, opens the door to other powers in the cosmos) and a worldview that makes God responsible for everything and struggles with the resultant conclusion that among God's works are sources of great anguish, this strand of traditional belief has chosen the latter. And although neither the Isaiah passage nor the Mishnah's directive requires us to celebrate or give thanks for the fact that God is sometimes the source of evil or harm, both do require that we acknowledge and accept the fact.[22] It seems only in relatively modern times that people have begun to adopt the view characterized by the statement "I could never believe in a God who would let _____ (fill in the blank with the natural disaster that you find most appalling) happen." Somewhere along the line, apparently, we began to take a more utilitarian, more self-serving, view of God and religion. As long as God was beneficial to *us*, we could accept God. Once God was linked to things that harmed us, or caused us pain, we rejected God.

This shift in philosophy, though commonplace, seems strange. After all, most people do not reject their children, even when their children do unpleasant or evil things. One regularly hears interviews with the mothers (interestingly, it seems rarely with fathers) of convicted criminals, even murderers, who say, "I know my child did something awful, but I still love him!" Yet many in today's world are not able to make the same statement about God. It seems that whereas our expectations of human beings (our children or others) are realistic, so that we do not reject them totally when they do bad things, our expectations of God, on the other hand, are highly unrealistic. In fact, if God, as I have argued, is to be found in the natural laws and forces that give structure, order, and beauty to the cosmos, then it is quite clear that those laws will sometimes—or often—create situations that are destructive to human life. To hate, or reject, God or nature for these harmful things is to have a wholly unjustified and dangerously arrogant sense of our own place in the universe. We are, after all, just one part, one very small part, of the incredibly huge and complex system that we call the cosmos. Contrary to the beliefs of the ancients, the universe does *not* revolve around us. To be angry at, or reject, a universe that sometimes causes us great pain is self-centered and childish.

If we can accept the notion that God creates all natural things, the good and the bad, it seems a relatively small step to imagine that God commands all things. Some of those commandments are good and just and righteous. Others are not. This must be so if, as I am claiming, the part of God that commands is the emergent function of the complex interaction of human consciousnesses. We know for certain that humans sometimes make good, kind, righteous laws, and that we sometimes make bad, cruel, and unjust ones. So it should not be hard to imagine that God's injunctions cover a similar range. Some mitzvot will require us to act ethically and kindly, while others will not.

I am well aware of how troubling this formulation is. It means that we have to give up the notion that God always and only commands that which is good and just. But as I pointed out above, we've already come to terms with the fact that not everything God creates is good and beneficial, so why should everything God commands be good and beneficial? Even more troubling, though, is the notion that we cannot simply follow the rules blindly and assume that our actions will therefore be good. It means that all of us are under the same moral pressure as were the soldiers tried at Nuremburg who were told that "following orders" was not an acceptable defense of unacceptable behavior, nor did it relieve them of responsibility. Rather, each of us bears full responsibility for our actions.

EATING THE FRUIT AND LEAVING THE GARDEN

Personal responsibility is the key to my entire understanding of mitzvot. Each of us must judge the morality, the rightness, of everything that we are commanded to do, and accept or reject the commandment based on our own honest appraisal of whether it is the right thing to do. This is an ancient Jewish idea, stretching all the way back to the story of the Garden of Eden. For me it is a most important and revealing story. Adam and Eve, newly created, have been given just one rule: Do not eat of the fruit of the tree in the middle of the garden. Urged on by the serpent, they break the rule. Many interpretive traditions see this as a failure, a sin, the "fall of man" (and woman) from their perfect state to a guilty state—in other words, a great human tragedy. I see it differently. Taking the story at face value, we see that the primordial couple is given only one rule. But how could they be expected to follow that rule? After all, according to the terms laid out in the text, they did not yet have the capacity to distinguish good from evil. That capacity would only be gained once they ate the fruit that they were warned not to eat. So how could they have been expected to "do the right thing" and follow the rule?

It is a commonplace of modern criminal law that if a defendant is judged to be unable to understand the difference between right and wrong, he or she cannot be held culpable for his or her actions. We regularly hear of perpetrators being confined to psychiatric hospitals for observation until the court decides if they are competent to stand trial. That competence primarily involves the ability to understand what is right and what is wrong. Without that ability our system says it is impossible to try a criminal in the usual fashion, since an individual without that ability is seen as not being responsible for his or her actions. It is one of the fundamental abilities in normal human beings. So Adam and Eve, before eating the fruit, were not yet fully human. They lacked the knowledge of good and evil and could only acquire it by eating the fruit. In fact, they *had* to eat the fruit. The whole thing was a set-up. God knew that these new creatures, in order to fulfill their destiny of being created in God's image, had to be moral actors, decision makers who could be relied upon to evaluate the quality of their own actions (and God's as well—that's part of the covenantal responsibility taken on by Abraham, which is why God tells him of the plan to destroy Sodom and Gomorrah in the first place). If we could not be held accountable, we would not be fully human. This claim is often met with an objection: If we needed the ability to distinguish right from wrong, why didn't God give it to us? Why instead did God actually forbid us from getting it and punish us when we did so? My answer is that when it comes to judging and evaluating good and evil, *we* must take responsibility for our judgments. Adam and Eve are symbols of humankind in general. The message of the story is that it was important for them/us to take responsibility for the decision to acquire the capability to distinguish good from evil, and to accept the consequences of that decision. Those consequences were not "punishment" in the usual sense, but simply the natural consequences that we normally refer to as "growing up." As long as they/we were in a child-like state of innocence, meaning a state in which they/we were not yet able to judge right and wrong, they/we were allowed to stay in the idyllic surroundings of a garden in which their/our every need was provided for. But as soon as they/we ate the fruit and acquired the mature capability to know the difference between right and wrong, they/we grew up. Growing up, as we all know, involves being on one's own and being responsible for providing for one's own needs. God could have refrained from creating the tree of knowledge of good and evil, or could have created it but hidden it behind a wall in some out-of-the-way corner of the garden, or even planted it *outside* the garden. Any of these strategies would have been effective in keeping humans innocent and child-like, wholly dependent on God to know what to do. But God chose none of these approaches. Instead God put it in the middle of the garden, made it quite attractive, pointed it out to Adam, and then warned him not to eat of its fruit. The only conclusion that I can reach from this is that God wanted—even needed—us to eat the fruit and gain the independent capacity to make moral judgments. God did not want us to be automata or puppets.

If we leave the story and return to reality, we recognize that we human beings are by nature moral decision makers. We are regularly faced with decisions about how to act and we know, when that occurs, that we can make a good choice or a bad choice. Usually, we know the difference clearly. Sometimes we make a bad choice anyway, and we know as we are making it—sometimes consciously and sometimes subconsciously—that we are making a bad choice, but we do it anyway because it will feel good, or it's easier, or it's fun, or the crowd is doing it, or an authority figure told us to do it. Or God told us to do it. But none of these excuses relieves us from the ultimate responsibility for the choices we have made.

WHEN RABBIS ARGUE, GOD IS THERE

Jewish law works in some very curious ways. First, it is traditionally ironed out in a process of argumentation sometimes called *pilpul*, which means hair-splitting, endless arguments over minute points of law. When President Bill Clinton was embroiled in the scandal over his relationship with White House intern Monica Lewinsky, at one point, while testifying before a grand jury in August 1998, he made the statement, "That depends on what the meaning of 'is' is." Now while many Americans found this comment ridiculous, lots of rabbis I know commented that this sort of legal hair-splitting is perfectly understandable in the Talmudic tradition. In fact, "pilpul" involves dissecting the meaning of words, actions, and laws, drawing ever-finer distinctions, and arguing not only about grand principles but also about the details upon which those principles are built.

Second, halakhic (that is, Jewish legal) arguments virtually never include claims about what God wants, requires, allows, or prohibits. In other words, although there is an underlying assumption somewhere deep in the system that the laws in question are divine in origin, no rabbi in a legal discussion will *ever* claim that this or that specific point reflects God's view. In other religious traditions—for example, in Evangelical Christian circles—one often hears claims about what God wants or requires. But when rabbis argue, be it about tiny procedural details (e.g., whether the use of the sticky tapes that secure disposable diapers constitutes "sewing" and is thus prohibited on Shabbat[23]) or about sweeping moral questions (e.g., the permissibility of abortion or of withdrawing life-support measures from a brain dead patient), they couch their arguments in terms of precedents and legal reasoning, *not* on what they believe to be God's opinion.

These two characteristics of traditional halakha and the process by which it is developed often lead those who are not sympathetic to the entire subject to dismiss the whole endeavor. "You see," they claim, "it's not really about following God's law at all. When did we get off track and forget that this way of life was supposed to be spiritual? When did it become all about the nitpicking arguments of men[24] who care more about silly details than real principles?" This sort of critique is quite common in the liberal Jewish world. It reflects an underlying belief that the broad, moral principles are the real crux of God's requirements of us as Jews, and that long, convoluted, "pilpulistic" arguments about the details reveal an inability to see the forest for the trees. It may even reflect an underlying sense (though I am not certain most people would articulate this consciously) that they would like to believe that the Creator of the universe cares in a principled way that we observe Shabbat, because it teaches us that work ought not to be worshipped and that time ought to be sanctified, but they cannot believe that the eternal, omnipotent ruler of the universe really cares about whether we use disposable diapers on Shabbat. It's a level of detail that strains credibility to the breaking point.

I understand these objections. After all, it's hard to understand how something as long lasting, inspiring, and spiritual as Judaism should obsess over disposable diapers. Jews have willingly given their lives over the centuries rather than abandon their Judaism. Can something so beautiful, so meaningful, really boil down to the sticky tape on diapers? I understand the rolling of the eyes and the dismissive snort of many liberal Jews. But I want to propose that seeing God-the-giver-of-the-Torah as an emergent phenomenon, the product of the interaction of a huge number of consciousnesses, can change the way we see this issue. If God's consciousness, God's Self emerges from the interaction of human selves the way an individual human consciousness or self emerges out of the interaction among the neurons of a brain, then the more intricate, creative, and detailed those interactions become, the more fully will the emergence occur. In other words, the maturation of such an emergence grows and deepens with the diversity and creativity of the interactions. The addition of many levels of detailed analysis, even about details that seem trivial, increases the depth, breadth, and sophistication of the overall process. Consider two examples that will illustrate that the more diverse, detailed, and complex the thought process becomes, the more sophisticated and principled the result will be. One example concerns an individual human self and the other a communal interaction.

The individual example starts with a newborn infant. The infant needs food—that is, feels hungry. At this early stage, however, it is likely that she cannot yet identify or abstract the notions of "feel" or "hungry" or, most importantly, even the notion of "I" as in "I feel hungry." Rather, her body needs food and her brain registers that elementary fact. She cries. Luckily for her (since she is completely unable to procure any food on her own) she has a mother and a father who are awakened at 3 a.m. by her wailing and groggily attend to her needs. When she has nursed, she feels better and shows this by calming down and, if her parents are lucky, by falling back to sleep.

Now let's look at that same individual 23 years later. She is sitting in the grad school library, working on a project. She yawns, then looks at her watch, and says to herself, "I'm starving. I need to take a break and get some dinner. But it's Tuesday and the library only stays open until 8:00 and it's 7:15 already. I have to get this paper written before tomorrow's seminar. If I work on it for another half-hour, I'll get all the research done, then I'll be able to take a break and really enjoy dinner. Maybe I'll go out to that new Thai place. Oh wait—I promised my roommate that we would eat together tonight and she hates Thai food. I guess it's pizza again, but I'm getting so bored with pizza. I wish she would be a bit more adventurous in her eating. I'll talk with her about it—give her some food for thought. Ha-ha. Bad pun! OK, back to work." This internal monologue, that might only take a brief moment and is completely familiar in its tone to so many of us, demonstrates a huge level of complexity, abstraction, and creativity. Our grad student who, 23 years ago, was only able to wail until her parents awoke and fed her, now realizes that she is hungry. But she also realizes that she must prioritize her activities to succeed in a goal—getting her paper written—and the process of setting priorities argues for her to delay eating. If she delays and finishes her work, she anticipates being able to enjoy the meal more. She would like to eat a certain kind of food but then remembers a commitment she made to a friend that will make it impossible to eat that kind of food. The friendship, and the promise to the friend, take precedence over the desire to eat Thai food, though she then muses that it would be better if her friend would try exotic new foods. She considers trying to help her friend change, then makes a bit of a joke, using a word-play in which the words do not mean at all what they would mean if taken literally. This brief moment of daydreaming and planning includes a huge number of mental connections, associations, and trains of thought. Concepts like "time," "time management," "friendship," "promises," and others are tremendously complex when compared to the thought processes of a newborn, which (as far as we know) are basically limited to "hungry," "cold," "uncomfortable," and "content." We recognize intuitively that the mental processes of the 23-year-old are more mature, more intricate, and more complex. We might characterize them as reflecting a far more developed and complex sense of self.

Our communal example comes from the Babylonian Talmud. Here is the text:

> Mishnah: A man should not open a bakery or a dyer's workshop or a cowshed under his neighbor's store-room. . . . Gemara: "A man should not open a bakery. . . ." A Tanna taught: If the cowshed is there before the store-room, it may be opened. Abaye asked the following questions: "If the owner of the

upper room has cleared out and swept the room in preparation for a storeroom, what is the ruling? If he has opened out a number of windows, what is the ruling? . . . If he builds a room on the roof, what is the ruling?" These questions must stand.[25]

The first part of the text, from the Mishnah, gives a very simple rule regarding what we moderns would call zoning restrictions—that is, restrictions on what kinds of businesses may or may not be established in a particular place. The general principle, although not articulated, seems to be that one may not open a type of business on the first floor of a two-story building that would cause damage (in the examples cited, damage by noxious odors or heat) to merchandise stored on the second floor.

The second section, taken from the Gemara, complicates the principle stated in the Mishnah by claiming that if the smelly business was there first, it may remain, even after a storeroom is opened above. In other words, the Mishnah's principle only applies if the storeroom was already in existence when another tenant proposed opening a smelly business on the first floor. But if the first floor was already in use as, say, a cowshed, it need not be closed merely because someone else wishes to open a storeroom above. Note that this opinion is attributed to a *Tanna*, a scholar of the era of the Mishnah. Thus the Gemara's first step in treating the Mishnah is to add a layer of complexity from the same era as the Mishnah. It then goes on to quote a series of questions in the name of Abaye, a Babylonian scholar of the late third and early fourth centuries. All of his questions try to get at the same issue—namely, when does a storeroom become a storeroom? If the downstairs restrictions only apply if a storeroom *already* exists upstairs, what stage of completion must the upstairs storeroom be in to block the establishment of a noxious business downstairs? Obviously, the restrictions apply if there is already a storeroom there with shelves stocked with fabric or food or other goods. But what if the upstairs is already being prepared for use as a storeroom, even though nothing yet is stored there? Do the restrictions apply if the second story is in the final stages of preparation for storage? What if it is being remodeled as a storeroom? And what if the second story doesn't even exist yet, but then the owner begins to create it (by building a room on the roof of a single story building)? We could add some additional questions to Abaye's list. Does the restriction apply no matter what is stored in the storeroom? That is, might there be some kinds of material that would not be affected by being stored above a cowshed or bakery and, if so, would the restrictions still apply? Might there be a way around the restrictions, perhaps by having the owner of the downstairs establishment install a ventilation system? Are the restrictions limited to establishments that produce noxious odors or heat, or do they apply to any sort of business that creates a potentially damaging effect on things stored upstairs? Who decides if the downstairs business is "too noxious" to be allowed under the upstairs business? The upstairs tenant? The landlord? The court? One needs only a bit of imagination to spin a broad web of other questions about this minor point of business/zoning law. And while some people will throw up their hands in impatient disgust at this legal nitpicking, I see in it a highly complex attempt to create a society in which commerce can thrive, businesses can coexist, and neighbors can be guided in their disputes by agreed-upon legal principles. It is significant that many American courts—including, most prominently, the U.S. Supreme Court—are not one-judge affairs, but are composed of numerous judges who, at some point in the analysis of a case, argue its fine points among themselves. This was certainly the case as well in ancient Jewish courts. The entire first section of the Mishnah's Tractate Sanhedrin is devoted to determining how many judges are needed to adjudicate various different types of cases. In that discussion the minimum number of judges required for the least important cases is three. There are cases that require five and cases that require seven, but the most serious cases require twenty-three judges. Why is this so? If a judge is very smart, highly experienced, and very wise, why not allow him[26] to hear cases by himself? The answer seems clear: No matter how wise an individual judge may be, greater wisdom will be found in the interaction among a group of judges. Given my claims about God's consciousness as the emergent function of the interaction among human consciousnesses, I would argue that *submitting a case to a panel of judges for their argumentation, analysis, and final disposition is tantamount to submitting the case for adjudication by God.*

This claim will certainly seem audacious if we examine it through the lens of a traditional theology in which God's judgments are perfect, true, and infallible, whereas we generally recognize that the best of human judgments is, in the final analysis, still human and therefore imperfect and flawed. But my claim all along has been that God's judgments, being the emergent property of human judgments, are just as imperfect as merely human judgments. Perhaps this is one of the more unsettling ramifications of the claim, made first in Genesis 1:26, that we humans are created *b'tselem Elohim*—in the image of God. This fundamental notion was understood by Abraham and Moses. It made them question the correctness and the justness of God's intentions and challenge God, even though they perceived that doing so could be a very risky business. We moderns would do well to take them as role models.

CHANGING THE LAW

The text of the Torah is quite explicit about the closed nature of the law. "Everything that I command you, that is what you shall take care to do: Do not add to it or take away from it."[27] Nevertheless, questions of when, how, and why we might in fact add to or take away from the law have long been subjects of debate within the Jewish community. The rabbis of the Talmudic era developed various means of adjusting the law without, in their eyes, violating the letter of the Torah's warning. So, for example, they developed standards for interpreting the Torah's laws in order to specify details that seem, to most observers, to be additions to or subtractions from the Torah's laws. A classic and common example is in the dietary laws. The Torah commands that we "not boil a kid in its mother's milk," and this is expanded by rabbinic interpretation to an absolute separation of all things dairy and all things meat. This was not seen as violating the Torah's principle since it was merely interpreting the Torah's words so as to provide a necessary level of detail. A more daring move was the institution of the *takkanah*, or rabbinic decree. These are rare cases in which great rabbis simply create new law in response to a pressing need among the people. A well-known example is the *prozbul*, an economic device attributed to the early first century scholar Hillel. In an era of increasing commercial dependence on credit, the Torah's rule that all debts were to be canceled in the seventh, or sabbatical (*shmitah*), year became a real hardship. Lenders were not inclined to extend loans in the fifth and sixth years, knowing that they would not be repaid. Hillel created a mechanism whereby loans could be transferred to the court just before the shmitah year, and transferred back to the individual creditors after the end of the year, thus allowing business to thrive. The logic was that the law of Deuteronomy required that "every creditor shall remit the due that he claims from his neighbor; he shall not dun his neighbor or kinsman,"[28] but the law did not apply to debts held by the court. A less well-known example (but one that is far more important in the lives of contemporary Jews) is the decree attributed to Rabbenu Gershom, a tenth century German scholar, prohibiting the biblically permitted practice of polygamy. In all these rabbinic cases, however, the rabbis are careful to maintain a clear sense that the Torah's laws are of divine origin and are, therefore, absolutely binding. The modifications that they enact are, in their eyes, merely interpretations and therefore well within their purview. The fact that the result of such interpretation is occasionally to radically change the apparent force of the Torah's law simply reveals to the rabbis how misleading a superficial reading of the law can be.

A different approach was taken in the modern era when scholars first began to recognize in Jewish legal tradition a mixture of divine and human elements. Many have adopted the attitude that we humans are not free to modify what God decreed, but are completely free to change that which was added by human beings. This leads to great debates over which core elements in a particular area of law are divine and which are the "accretions" that have built up over the generations of Jewish history. Great care must be taken with the former, while the latter may be modified with more flexibility. A more radical approach in the modern world has been to say that the entire corpus of law is human, from beginning to end. These laws are to be regarded with great reverence, for they have created the infrastructure that has kept the Jewish people alive and allowed it to thrive. However, when necessary they may be changed or set aside, especially when doing so will strengthen or protect the welfare of the people. Human beings created them in the first place, so human beings can feel comfortable changing them.

These modern approaches have led to a wide array of Jewish practices and attitudes towards the law. Some Jews observe what they call "biblical kashrut," for example, in which they follow the dietary laws as laid down in the Bible but not the Talmudic developments that gave those laws most of what we know as their traditional content. They refrain from eating prohibited species (e.g., pork and shellfish) but do not follow the intricate laws regarding the separation of dairy foods and meat foods. Such a practice seems to stem from a belief that the biblical level of the laws is divine, while the postbiblical developments are not.

Seeing God-the-lawgiver as an emergent phenomenon brings a new light to the entire question of the origin of Jewish law and our rationale for deciding when to observe and when to abandon or modify the mitzvot. On the one hand, the mitzvot are clearly of human origin. Not a single one was revealed by an eternal, supernatural force that created the universe. From the most reasonable social laws prohibiting murder and theft, to the most arcane and nonintuitive laws requiring the wearing of ritual tassels[29] or prohibiting the weaving together of linen and wool,[30] they are all of human origin. On the other hand, their development in a social context involving the interconnection among many minds over many centuries means that they are the product of an emergent consciousness—that is, they are divine. But, finally, this fact does not in any way make them unquestionable, immutable, or absolute. Rather, we are obligated to evaluate and judge them, and to make responsible decisions about whether and how to observe the mitzvot. Given the properties of emergence, we may even say that the longer these laws are studied, discussed, and thought about in community (even if the study and discussion lead to modification), the more divine they become.

AN IDEAL APPROACH TO PICKING AND CHOOSING

Traditional Jews sometimes criticize Liberal Jews for picking and choosing—that is, making a case-by-case decision about which mitzvot to follow and which to reject or ignore. They argue that the mitzvot come as a system, a package, given entirely by God (or by the rabbis, or by "tradition") and that it is not our right to decide which ones are worthy of our obedience and which are not. It should be obvious by this point that I do not share either of the elements of this critical view. I do not see all the mitzvot as a single package that operates on a take-it-or-leave-it basis. I do not believe that any system of law constitutes a unitary package: we make decisions in every area of law regarding which laws to obey, which to break, and which to ignore. But more importantly, I believe that it is not only our right but our obligation to evaluate the mitzvot and make decision about which ones to follow. This is what it means to take responsibility for our actions, rather than ceding responsibility to some larger power and thereby seeking refuge under its wings when we perform a commanded act that we know to be wrong.

I differ with many Liberal Jews, however, on one very important point. For quite a while now, Liberal Judaism in various forms has celebrated the individual and individual autonomy (sometimes referred to as personal autonomy) as the highest expressions of our humanness, and has urged each of us to pick and choose among the offerings of Jewish tradition based on our own personal, individual judgments. We are encouraged to make religious decisions that will create a rich and meaningful Jewish life for ourselves, as individuals. Consider the following excerpts from the opening pages of Rabbi Morrison Bial's *Liberal Judaism at Home: The Practice of Modern Reform Judaism*, first published in 1967:

> [T]he majority of Liberal Jews feel that any establishment of standards would lead to regimentation and would deny individual responsibility, which has always been the touchstone of the Liberal Jew. Also, any such code, no matter how vaguely worded, would set limits to individual decision. . . .
> [W]hat can the Liberal Jew use as his final criterion . . .? The answer must be a sense of *kedushah,* of holiness, of that which will help him sanctify his life, to make it truly meaningful.[31]

Somewhat more recently, prominent Reform thinkers have backed away from personal autonomy as an absolute value, calling for it to be balanced by the voice of tradition. So, for example, in 1983 Rabbi Eugene Borowitz wrote that "postmodern liberal Jewish thought needs to be fully dialectical. It should not make Judaism subservient to a truth derived from the culture, as the old liberals did, yet it should not require the sacrifice of personal autonomy to the Torah, as Orthodoxy still demands."[32] And just a few years later, we find the following in an address entitled "Personal Autonomy and the Sense of Mitzvah," delivered by Rabbi Peter Knobel to the assembled members of the Central Conference of American Rabbis, or CCAR (the membership organization of North American Reform rabbis): "What I am suggesting is not the abandonment but the tempering of autonomy. By emphasizing community, we de-emphasize the isolated individual and we express a bias toward the collective wisdom of the community."[33]

And finally, in 1999 the CCAR voted on a "statement of principles" that seems (perhaps deliberately) to obscure any clear view regarding the status, the importance, and the authority of Jewish law:

> We cherish the truths revealed in Torah, God's ongoing revelation to our people and the record of our people's ongoing relationship with God. . . .
> We are called by Torah to lifelong study in the home, in the synagogue and in every place where Jews gather to learn and teach. Through Torah study we are called to mitzvot, the means by which we make our lives holy.
> We are committed to the ongoing study of the whole array of mitzvot and to the fulfillment of those that address us as individuals and as a community. Some of these mitzvot, sacred obligations, have long been observed by Reform Jews; others, both ancient and modern, demand renewed attention as the result of the unique context of our own times.[34]

These statements, and numerous others like them, seek to blunt the focus on personal autonomy and bring it into more balance with communal norms or communal wisdom. However, they do so largely out of a sense that modernity has shown the individual self to have a pretty poor record of rational, moral excellence and out of a concern that purely personal decision making will lead to a Jewish life governed by convenience and whim rather than by appreciation for tradition or spiritual values. On the other hand, I am suggesting that the advantage gained by emphasizing communal study, discussion, and decision making lies not in the tendency of these processes to keep Jews more firmly attached to Jewish tradition (though they most certainly do that), but rather in the connectedness of community to the divine. When community wrestles with interpretations of mitzvot, God is there and the decisions reached are essentially what were historically thought of as revelation. This does not mean that the decisions are always right, true, or just, nor does it relieve the individual from the obligation to evaluate them. But unlike the modern liberal tradition that has often seen both Jewish tradition and divine revelation as being in tension with the individual mind, the paradigm I am proposing sees the divine as emerging out of the interactions among individual minds—in other words, out of community.

NOTES

1. I generally avoid using such traditional, gendered pronouns when referring to God, but here I am referring to a God-narrative that is ancient and not at all egalitarian. It seems clear that the God of the Torah is considered to be a powerful masculine figure.
2. Ex. 20:2–3.
3. Lev. 19:37.
4. Deut. 13:1.
5. The Talmud is composed of the Mishnah and the Gemara.
6. Pirkei DeRabbi Eliezer chap. 46.
7. Moses Maimonides's Introduction to his *Mishneh Torah*. The translation is my own.

8. I do not include Reconstructionists, Renewal, Humanists, or other small groupings here in part because they comprise such a small percentage of the Jewish world, and in part because they are less susceptible to the crude categorization by level of observance that I am describing. In no way do I mean to imply that they are unimportant. Indeed, in some ways the fact that they do not fit into the crude categorization makes them more interesting to me.

9. Joseph Stein, *Fiddler on the Roof* (New York: Crown Publishers, 1964), 2.

10. This extreme case raises another serious moral question—namely, why would someone beg his or her beloved to do something that was so distasteful? Ought not mutual love lead each party never to want to force the other to do something unpleasant? These questions go to the heart of what might be called the morality of love. Their application to the whole issue of God's covenant with the people of Israel is a most challenging theological topic.

11. Bereshit Rabbah 1:4.
12. Babylonian Talmud, Bava Metzia 59b.
13. Deut. 30:12.
14. Ps. 19:7–9.
15. Gen. 18:23–25.
16. Ex. 32:10.
17. Ex. 32:11–13.
18. Ex. 4:10.

19. Raphael Patai, *Gates to the Old* City (Detroit: Wayne State University Press, 1981), 729. In his notes Patai cites as the source of the story Yitzchaq Ashkenazi, *Otzrot fun Idishen Humor* [Treasuries of Jewish Humor] (New York: Tel Aviv Publishers, 1929), 20.

20. Isa. 45:7.

21. Berakhot 9:4. It is in the same section of the Mishnah that we first hear of the tradition of reciting a specific blessing—namely, "Blessed is God, the Judge of Truth [*Dayan ha-emet*]" on sad occasions, as for example when hearing of a death.

22. Many people assume that the recitation of a blessing is a form of thanksgiving. This is a widespread misunderstanding. Although there are blessings that specifically offer thanks to God, most blessings simply acknowledge God's role in whatever process or event is the blessing's subject, raising our awareness of the connection between the event and God but by no means expressing gratitude for it.

23. See J. David Bleich, "The Use of Disposable Diapers on Shabbat." *Journal of Halacha and Contemporary Society* (1986), vol. XII, 27–49.

24. Note that the fact that the halakhic system has, for the vast bulk of its history, been a male-dominated system is a salient point for some modern liberal critics.

25. Babylonian Talmud, Bava Batra 20b.

26. In a modern American context, I would say "him or her," but rabbinic law allowed only men to be judges.

27. Deut. 13:1.
28. Deut. 15:2.
29. *Tzitzit*. See Num. 15:37–41.
30. *Shatnez*. See Lev. 19:19.

31. Morrison David Bial, *Liberal Judaism at Home: The Practice of Modern Reform Judaism* (New York: Union of American Hebrew Congregations, 1971), 4, 8–9.

32. Eugene B. Borowitz, *Choices in Modern Jewish Thought: A Partisan Guide* (New York: Behrman House, 1983), 267.

33. Peter Knobel, "Personal Autonomy and the Sense of Mitzvah," in *Central Conference of American Rabbis Yearbook*. Vol. XCVI, 1987, 42.

34. "A Statement of Principles for Reform Judaism." Adopted in Pittsburgh at the 1999 Convention of the Central Conference of American Rabbis.

Chapter Five

Scrutinizing the Model

My purpose throughout this book has been to propose a new, rational way of thinking about or imagining God as being conscious and sentient. In the foregoing chapters, I described God's consciousness as the emergent effect of the complex interaction among a very large number of human (and perhaps nonhuman) consciousnesses. The question now is how good a model is this, by which I mean, "How well does the model stand up to scrutiny? How convincingly does it respond to some of the basic questions that are often posed to systematic theological models?" In particular, I want to address three specific questions. In the model described here:

- Does God have a will?
- Does God intervene in history?
- How might prayer function?

DOES GOD HAVE A WILL?

It is quite clear that the Big Bang and the laws of nature have no will, no desire. They simply exist. They determine quite literally the shape of our universe, but they cannot decide to act or to refrain from acting. Thus the first part of my answer to this question is that the stage of God that was responsible for the development of the universe up until the evolution of consciousness, perhaps the first 13 billion years, did not have will. Will is clearly a function of mind and before there is mind there can be no will. So, contrary to the vast majority of traditional Jewish thinkers, I would argue that God did not *will* the creation to occur, but rather that it was simply in the nature of God—the sum total of the natural laws in the cosmos—to exist and to drive the existence of all nonsentient realities, including space, time, energy, and the matter of stars, planets, galaxies, and so on. The question changes, however, once sentience evolves in the universe and God then becomes sentient as the emergent result of that evolution. Then we must ask whether God, as a conscious entity, has a will.

The answer to this question is quite clear in ancient Jewish text. There God is portrayed unequivocally as having a will. God chooses to behave in certain ways and responds volitionally to various human circumstances and actions. God initially decided to create the world, although the biblical text is curiously silent about the details of this decision. As the narrative develops, however, we are told clearly that God decided in a most deliberative fashion to create human beings. In the first creation narrative, God says, "Let us make the human in our image, after our likeness,"[1] and in the second God says, "It is not good for the human to be alone. I shall make a helper to complement him."[2] When human behavior becomes corrupted, the text tells us that "the Eternal regretted that He had made the humans in the earth, and His heart was saddened. The Eternal said, 'I shall wipe out the humans that I created from the face of the earth—humans and beasts and crawling things and birds of the sky—for I regret that I made them.'"[3] These and many other examples clearly portray God as having will.

But does it make sense for me to think of God as having a will based on the way I have described God's consciousness? In order to answer the question, we must turn briefly to one of the toughest scientific and philosophical issues ever to confront human thinkers—namely, the nature of free will. It is quite clear that we *think* we have freedom to choose the course of our lives and that we make decisions volitionally, but it is not clear that our perception of freedom matches reality. Some have claimed that our sense of freedom is illusory. Let's consider two examples, one trivial and one far more weighty. I wake up in the morning and prepare to dress for my day. I have a sense that I am *choosing freely* what I will wear. Jeans and a t-shirt? Or a dress shirt, tie, khakis, and a sport coat? I seem to choose the latter freely. Another example: My wife and I were cruising through life in our mid-thirties. We had careers, half-finished doctoral dissertations, a home, and two wonderful sons. We thought and discussed and weighed our options, and then *decided* to have a third child.

These two examples are typical of the decisions that we humans make throughout our lives. Most often we have the sense that we make them freely. But there are those who claim that at any decision-making point, our genetic makeup and the sum total of all our prior experiences—the things we've learned, the earlier decisions we've made, the people with whom we associate, the values and mores of the society in which we live, and countless other factors—conspire to force our hand. It *feels* like we're making autonomous, free decisions, but really we are "programmed" as a result of all our experiences to make whatever decision we end up making. It's a fascinating and sobering claim. From inside my sense of self, I always think that I am making a free choice and that I could reverse my decision, choosing the jeans and t-shirt or choosing not to have another child. From another person's perspective, however, the choice I would make seems obvious. We have all had the experience of knowing others (our children, for example) very well and watching them make decisions, then saying to ourselves, "I knew she would choose Harvard over Michigan (or the jeans over the dress, or marrying now instead of waiting another five years, or whatever). It was impossible for her to make any other decision!" What we mean is that based on our knowledge of an individual and that person's prior decisions, we were certain that he or she would decide in a particular way, and in fact that was the outcome. So which is it? Do we choose freely or is our sense of freedom an illusion?

Unfortunately, the most definitive thing that can be said in response to this difficult question is that it *seems* to me that I *do* have free will. That is to say that although there is no way in the world to *prove* that I have free will, I *believe* that I do. It *feels* as if I do. My *experience* of consciousness, of what it is like to be Me, is consistent with personal freedom. So far, although many theorists have tried, no one has demonstrated how human free will might work—that is, what the mechanism might be. If we start with the notion of the conscious self as the emergent property of the huge and highly complex interconnections among neurons, and we consider that each of those neurons is essentially a simple switch that either stays off or turns on depending on the inputs it receives, it is hard to imagine a mechanism whereby this system could *choose* a t-shirt over a dress shirt.[4] Nevertheless, when I get dressed in the morning, it *seems* to me that I make a decision, and my decision does not seem to be solely the result of a complex series of neural switches staying off or turning on as a result of the inputs they receive from other neural switches.

Some have claimed that at the heart of the free decision-making process is quantum uncertainty. On the smallest scale of reality, things do not happen in predictable ways; rather, there is a strong element of utter randomness, a roll of the dice, in determining the future state of a system.[5] But this explanation still violates our sense that we make free choices in a deliberate manner. Whether my choice is determined by a vast conspiracy of past experiences or by a random event in the subatomic structure of my brain at the quantum level, I am still left with the experience that my choice is not determined by anything—except Me.

This belief that we choose freely is more than just a philosophical curiosity. It stands at the very heart of human society. It would not be possible for any human civilization to operate under a system of laws if we did not start with the unshakeable assumption that we choose freely to act in any way at any point. The whole notion of responsibility is critically dependent on this assumption. If a person is lying in bed in the middle of the night and a freak windstorm uproots a tree outside and the tree falls on the house and kills the unfortunate person, we regard it as a tragedy but not a crime. If, however, a thief breaks into the house and in the course of the robbery kills the homeowner, we hold the thief responsible. Windstorms and trees are not held responsible for the damage they inflict, but human beings are. The difference lies in our assumption that humans have free will. Neither the wind nor the tree chooses how it will behave, but people do. Therefore we can prosecute people for making wrong or immoral or destructive choices.

Jewish tradition is no less committed to the belief that we humans have free will. The Torah is rooted in the notion of an all-powerful God of Heaven and Earth who, one might think, could certainly control human behavior as easily as He controls the weather, splits seas, or rains down fire and brimstone on sinful cities. Yet the biblical God seems unwilling to exert control over human will.[6] Especially in the covenantal relationship between God and Israel, free will seems to be the rule. We read in Deuteronomy, "I call heaven and earth to witness against you today. I set before you life and death, blessing and curse. Choose life, that you and your descendants might live."[7] The theme recurs throughout the Bible. God offers us potential rewards—large population, safety and security, a land of promise and plenty, long life, and more—on condition that we follow a set of divine laws. Such a quid pro quo can only be based on the notion of free will.

The rabbis who crafted the contours of postbiblical Jewish belief were also deeply committed to the assumption that we are free. *Pirkei Avot* tells us that "all is foreseen, but freedom is given,"[8] a sentiment that seems to prefer the paradoxical coexistence of complete divine foreknowledge and complete human freedom to the tidier philosophical situation that would have prevailed had the rabbis been willing to give up either side of the equation. The Talmud reinforces the sense of our free will in the statement "Everything is in the hands of Heaven—except fear of Heaven."[9] That is to say, God controls everything except our obedience to God. The sages even object to the possibility that God may exert pressure to limit human freedom (as opposed to suspending it altogether). In a well-known Talmudic passage considering the terrifying circumstances surrounding the biblical account of the giving of the Torah at Sinai (the mountain smoking and trembling, loud blasts of a shofar, and so on), the rabbis say that it was as if "the Holy Blessed One overturned the mountain and suspended it upon them like a barrel and said to them: 'If you accept the Torah, well and good, but if not—there shall be your burial!' Rabbi Aha ben Jacob observed: 'This furnishes a strong protest against the Torah' [i.e., a blanket excuse for nonobservance of a covenant ratified under duress]."[10] Thinking like lawyers, the rabbis are deeply disturbed by the possibility that the covenant between God and Israel might have been executed under circumstances of duress, thereby undermining its authority. They resolve these concerns by pointing to the events recounted in the book of Esther. There the Jews of Persia lived in an environment that appeared to offer every incentive *not* to be a Jew, since Haman had plotted to kill all Jews. Yet the Jews chose to maintain their Jewish identity nonetheless. This choice was clearly without duress and the rabbis see this as the solution to the problem of coercion at Sinai. For them a covenant that is not freely chosen is deeply flawed.

In medieval Jewish philosophy, the existence of human freedom is seen as a question of moral logic, rather than divine ability. In other words, it is not a question of whether God might be able to suspend human freedom or control human actions, but rather of what the moral consequences of such divine control would be. Maimonides makes a very clear statement in his code of law:

> 1. Freedom is given to every human. If one wishes to steer oneself on a good path and be righteous, one is free to do so. And if one wishes to steer oneself on an evil path and to be wicked, one is free to do so. This is the meaning of the Torah verse, ". . . now the human has become like one of us, knowing good and evil . . . ." (Gen. 3:22). In other words, this species, humans, has become unique in the world, and there is no other species like it in so far as it distinguishes good and bad based on its own wisdom and thinking. It [i.e., the human species] does everything it wants, and there is none who can prevent it from doing good or evil. And because it is thus, ". . . and lest he reach out [and take and eat from the Tree of Life and live forever]" (Genesis 3:22 continued).
> 2. Do not even think about what the ignorant pagans and most of the simpletons among the Jews say, that the Holy Blessed One decrees for each human from his creation whether he will be righteous or wicked. That is not the way it is. Rather, each human is free to be as righteous as Moses our Teacher or as wicked as Jeroboam, or wise or foolish or merciful or cruel. . . . And there is none who can coerce him or decree upon him or pull him towards one of these paths except himself. . . .
> 4. If God had decreed that humans be righteous or wicked, or had put in place something that would pull a human, as an inborn trait, to one path or another . . . (as the ignoramuses wrongly claim), then how could it be a mitzvah for us from the prophets to do thus and not do thus or take the good path and do not follow your wickedness if it were decreed from creation or if there were an inborn trait pulling us to something from which it was impossible to move? And what would be the place of the whole Torah? And how would it be just and fair that the wicked be punished for wickedness or the righteous rewarded for righteousness? "Will the Judge of all the earth not act justly?" (Gen. 18:25).[11]

This passage goes on quite a bit in the original, with disparaging slurs cast at the "ignorant" and "stupid" who believe that our choices are not free. The passion of Maimonides's opinion makes sense, for as a rationalist he was deeply committed to the notion that God rules us rationally through the laws of the Torah. He believed deeply that the universe and the God who rules it are rational, and thus he could not fathom why any system of law would exist if we were not free to obey or transgress the laws. Essentially this is an ethical argument for human free will. If God gives us laws, and rewards and punishes us for obeying or transgressing those laws, then either we must be free to choose to obey or transgress or else God's system of reward and punishment must be arbitrary and unjust. This latter conclusion was unthinkable to Maimonides, and so he had no choice but to assume the former—namely, that we choose freely how to behave.

Thus, despite the apparent inability of modern neuroscientists and philosophers to explain *how* we can make free choices, the fact remains that we humans have the sense that our choices are indeed free, that we have and exercise will. Jewish tradition endorses this view and sets it as a cornerstone for the covenantal relationship between God and the people of Israel.

If individual human beings have will that they can freely exercise, and if God's consciousness (that is to say, God's Self) is the emergent property of the vast number and intricate complexity of interactions among all human consciousnesses, then it must follow that God has free will also. After all, just as it is commonplace for us to experience the expression of an individual's will, it is similarly commonplace to observe the expression of the will of a unit of social interaction—for example, a couple, a family, or a mob. Here I am not referring to the decision reached by a majority vote that is then declared to be the will of the group. Rather, I am thinking of situations where, without anything as formal or structured as a vote, a group simply expresses its clear will *as* a group to behave in one way rather than another. This expression of will arising from an interaction among individuals is an example of the expression of God's will, becoming more and more divine (as it were) the larger the group and the more complex its interactions. If we have free will, then so does God.

But that is not the end of the question. It is, in fact, just the easy beginning. The hard part comes when we ask, "So what? What does the existence of divine will *mean* for us? What effect or impact does it or should it have?" In the traditional paradigm, where God was seen as the omnipotent, omniscient, supernatural King of Kings, the answer to these questions was obvious. It was our human responsibility, as servants of God, to do God's will more or less unquestioningly. So in the services of Rosh Hashanah and Yom Kippur, there is a series of paragraphs that begin with the word *U-v'khen* ("and therefore"). The very first one begins as follows: "And therefore, Eternal our God, place the fear of You on all those You have made and the awe of You on all those You have created. All those You have made will revere You, and all creatures shall bow before You. And all will be united as a group *to do Your will with a whole heart*"[12] [emphasis added]. Clearly, the *teshuvah,* or "repentance," called for on these sacred days involves giving up the pursuit of one's own will and deciding instead to follow God's will. The underlying assumption is that there is a tension between my will and God's will. The message of the day-long liturgy of atonement is that my will leads me to the sinful path of seeking pleasure, personal gain, and the like, while God's will would have me choose the righteous path of pursuing justice, helping others, and so on. The notion is reinforced in Pirkei Avot: "Make His [God's] will like your will, so that God will make your will like His will. Nullify your will before His will, so that He will nullify the will of others before your will."[13] The meaning is clear: God's will—that is, what God wishes to accomplish—comes to pass; nothing else can be counted upon. A final illustration of the notion of divine will comes in a short Hebrew formula, just three words, that is used often in ritual and communal circumstances. The words are *Ken yehi ratzon* (So may it be [God's] will). Rabbis often use the formula to close sermons or impromptu prayers, and it is customary for the congregation to intone these words after each of the three lines of the traditional priestly blessing. The words mean simply, "Let it be so," but the language refers to God's will. A colloquial version of this is the English expression "God willing," which is used by many (especially in the culture of the more observant Jewish community) as a customary add-on to any statement about future plans. "Next year, God willing, we're going to redo the kitchen." Or "After I finish this course, God willing, I'll only have to write my thesis before I graduate." Again, God's will is understood as ultimately controlling everything that occurs in the world. My intentions *may* have an impact, but God's most certainly will.

None of this is revolutionary or new or surprising. These are some of the oldest and simplest assumptions of traditional Jewish belief. The problem is that I can't accept them, nor can many other contemporary Jews. That is, after all, what has brought me to this point of rethinking how I can imagine God's Self. I am incapable of believing that there is a supernatural Being out there who has the final say in whether I will redo my kitchen. But having defined God's will as emerging from the complex expression of will generated by intricately interconnected communities of people, ultimately the interconnectedness of *all* people, what can we say about this understanding of God's will? First of all, unlike the traditional religious understanding of God's will, it does not always come to fruition. We are *not* all-powerful and cannot control our world absolutely. Sometimes we humans are remarkable in our tenacity, our determination, and our ability to overcome huge odds in our attempts to implement our will. But often, no matter how hard we try, we simply fail. It is one of the most basic realities of life. So God's will, the emergent expression of the interacting wills of all the consciousnesses that exist, is essentially limited.

Second, and more disturbing to those who cherish traditional beliefs, if God's will is the emergent expression of the complex interactions of a huge number of human wills, then it cannot be counted on to be right, good, just, or moral. It will probably exhibit those qualities roughly as often as individual human beings or small groups of human beings do—which is to say, sometimes but not always. And certainly not often enough (or reliably enough) to allow us safely to say, with traditional pietists, that we should follow God's will instead of our own in all circumstances. Ultimately, the same responsibility that rests on our shoulders to judge the rightness or wrongness of God's laws weighs just as heavily upon us to judge the rightness or wrongness of God's will. This seemingly arrogant stance actually enhances the meaning of the covenant between God and Israel. That our traditional texts chose to frame our relationship with God primarily as a covenant, implying reciprocity and mutual obligation and responsibility, implies a certain significant level of trust in the human capacity for moral reasoning. God is not portrayed in those texts as wanting Israel to be a puppet, but rather a partner—if perhaps a junior partner. As such, it is our obligation to express our judgment of God's will, rather than accepting it uncritically as always right.

Before we leave the issue of God's will, I want to suggest one more understanding of the concept. It may be that when we invoke God's will we are using it as a term to label "that which is right and good," rather than really meaning that it is the actual will of a supernatural supreme Being. In that case "God's will" is simply code for "the will to do right." I suspect that many people, if they think deeply and honestly about their own beliefs, may in fact be using the concept in this fashion. But I take quite seriously the notion that God's existence is real, although my claim that God's self is an emergent property of many interconnected human consciousnesses means that it is somehow rooted in human beings. God really *does* have a will. That will is not omnipotent, however. It can guide human behavior but, like all human wills, its guidance is not to be trusted blindly, but rather judged carefully and critically.

DOES GOD INTERVENE IN HISTORY?

In *Judaism, Physics and God*, I proposed that along with the traditional notions of God as Judge, Shepherd, Parent, King, and so on, we add to our repertoire of God-metaphors the notion of God as Big Bang. But there is a problem with this metaphor. The Big Bang happened only once. Its tremendous influence on all future states of the universe results from its initial occurrence and the physical laws and processes that then took over. Even though the "echo" of the Big Bang still "reverberates"[14] in the universe today (in the form of energy known as the "cosmic background radiation"), the event only happened at the very beginning of the life of our universe. The Big Bang does not intervene in history. It does not save us from disaster or suspend its natural laws from time to time in miraculous ways to help us prevail over crises.

But traditional Judaism is profoundly dependent on a belief that God *does* intervene in history. This message is drummed into us through our annual festival cycle. We begin with Passover's commemoration of God's redemption of our ancestors from Egyptian slavery; we move on to Shavuot, marking God's revelation of the Torah to our people at Mount Sinai; and we conclude with Sukkot, when we remember the shelter God provided us during the forty years in the desert. Each of these events was portrayed as an instance of God intervening in human history, making important changes at crucial moments in order to guide the trajectory of our people's journey. Rabbinic tradition decreed that both Hannukah and Purim be observed with the recitation of the prayer *Al Ha-Nissim* ("For the miracles and the redemption and the acts of might and the salvation and the [victory in] wars that You performed for our ancestors in those days at this season"), since these holidays involved God's miraculous intervention to redeem the Jews from the existential threat of Hellenism and Persian genocide, respectively. This liturgical practice is somewhat surprising since God's intervention is not explicitly mentioned in either story. In Purim it is well known and often pointed out that the name of God does not appear even once in the book of Esther. In fact, it seems, based on a simple reading of the book, that the salvation of the Jews came about entirely as the result of the courage and cleverness of Esther and Mordechai. But the rabbis insist that God's hand was involved in the miracle, albeit as a hidden force. Likewise, in the Hannukah story it is often noted that although the conflict between Maccabees and Syrians, or Maccabees and Hellenized Jews, occurred in the early second century BCE, the story of the miraculous jar of oil that burned for eight days—even though it should have lasted for just one—did not appear until at least the fourth century CE. The rabbis seem to have inserted God's salvation into both stories. They did so because they *needed* to see a divine hand moving in these otherwise rather secular stories of political intrigue and military conflict. Indeed, it is virtually impossible to imagine the broad sweep of Jewish thought, Jewish belief, or Jewish literature without a belief that God intervenes in history, jumping in to alter the course of events so that The Plan can be followed.

But neither the Big Bang, nor the complexities of chaos theory, nor the random events of quantum mechanics intervene. They have no plan. They simply exist, driving reality inexorably with their unbreakable rules. Light always travels at a constant speed. Space time is always curved by the presence of mass or energy—resulting in what we know as gravity. Exceptions are never made, no matter how righteous the cause or deserving the supplicant.

So now we must ask, "Does God's conscious Self, that sentient force that I have described as the emergent result of the hugely complex interaction of a vast number of consciousnesses, intervene in history?" The answer will be similar to the answer to the question of whether this God has a will—namely, "Yes, but . . ." How so? We humans clearly intervene in history. The essential meaning of the claim that we have free will is that we have the power to intervene in history—in fact, to create history. When I look back on my life I see it as a series of choices, large and small. Who I am and what I have become are to a great extent the result of the choices I have made. I am satisfied with most of those choices. Some of them I regret. And it's important to realize that I made some decisions because I had to, without a clear or complete knowledge of how they would work out. That's what being human, and having only limited knowledge of the facts, involves. Finally, it is clear that some elements in my history have been (and continue to be) completely beyond my control. This is the landscape of the history of individual human lives. We make decisions to control many elements of our developing history. Some work out well, others do not. And some things are beyond our control. So on an individual level we may say that we do intervene in history, though we cannot count on our intervention being successful all the time.

You might object, "That's not intervening in history. That's just living your life and making decisions." My point is that this is exactly what history is made of. People live their lives and make decisions. Sometimes things work out the way they wish, while at other times their attempts at creating successful outcomes fail. And some forces of reality, especially some natural forces, cannot be overcome. One of the problems encountered in asking "Does God intervene in history?" is that the question implies that "history" is an independent force, a script that is being played out by actors who have no choice but to read their lines. Given that sense of history, intervening is often understood to mean what would happen if one of the actors, or perhaps the director, were to stand up in the middle of Act Two and shout, "Wait a minute! Hold on! Change that! Let's not have that character die. Let's have him recover, then leave his wife and join a commune in New Hampshire." This is essentially what the ancient Greek playwrights did by invoking the deus ex machina, literally the "god out of the machine." This was a device in Greek theater whereby if the plot had painted itself into a corner and there was no easy way to resolve the issue, a "machine" (a basket on ropes and pulleys) would be lowered from the top of the stage with a god in it who could intervene, magically solving the plot problem and allowing the play to end. But that's not the way we experience life. There is no predetermined script that is followed until and unless someone (or Someone) has the chutzpah and/or the wisdom to decide to change it. There are quite a few uncontrollable elements in life. We are born with a certain genetic endowment that may strongly influence or limit our abilities. We are affected by natural forces such as climate, disease, and random accidents, not to mention the cultural contexts in which we are raised. But we also make a large number of decisions that shape our lives. This is what free will is all about.

What we must do is change the question. Rather than asking whether God intervenes in history, we should ask whether God acts or has a role to play in history. That makes it sound less like there's a script and more as if history is the sum total of all the uncontrollable forces in life, plus all the decisions that are made. In my life I make many decisions, but other parts of my history are affected by decisions made by others, including my family members, those who have sat on admissions committees of schools I have attended (and schools I have not attended), employers who hired me (and potential employers who did not), etc. We might also say that History with a capital "H" (that is, the history of societies, nations, and the world, as opposed to the lower-case "h" history of you or me as individuals), operates in a similar way. It is made up of and influenced by some uncontrollable factors and many, many decisions made by a large number of individuals and groups. Now the question is "Does God also play a role in shaping history and, if so, what kind of a role is it?"

If we think of God's active, conscious Self as the emergent property of all the interacting conscious selves in the universe, then the answer is most certainly yes. Understood this way, God has a profound influence on history. The simplest form of such influence can perhaps be seen in our early childhood. I have a distinct memory from my early years, when I was perhaps seven or eight, of two different kinds of powerful social interactions. One is a memory of several occasions when my sister was caring for me while our parents were out, and we would come up with a great idea—to clean up the house, or make dinner, or do something else really grand. The idea developed between us in the form of "Let's surprise Mom and Dad when they get home!" Mind you, this didn't happen very often, but the few times it did left a deep impression on me, because the interaction between us produced behavior—history, if you will—that would likely not have occurred had I been by myself. A more frequent example involves the kind of situation where a bunch of kids were playing without enough adult supervision and the play got out of hand. Before you knew it, someone had been hurt, or something had been broken, or the group had made a disastrous decision (keep in mind that "disastrous" for 9-year-olds can be pretty minor), and none of it would ever have happened if I had been playing alone. In interactions these things build, grow, and take on a life of their own, for good and for bad. In the same way that divine law reduced to its simplest form is what happens when two people interact and produce law together (as opposed to one individual decreeing law), so divine influence on history in its simplest form occurs whenever the course of human events is affected by the emergent behavior of the members of even a small group interacting.

It is easy to extrapolate from my two childhood examples to what happens on a local, national, or global level. Large numbers of individuals interact in increasingly complex ways to produce both mass movements to improve the world and riots that can destroy it. The mass movement to demand civil rights for African Americans in the 1960s was a great example of improvement. People were inspired (the common use of the word is perhaps a clue that in fact God's influence was present) to behave in ways they would never have dreamed of if they acted alone, and to act with courage and grace that could only have resulted from the interaction of a mass movement. Images of Dr. Martin Luther King, Jr. and Rabbi Abraham Joshua Heschel marching together, or of thousands of people standing together singing "We Shall Overcome," have become icons of the period's history. On the other hand, the equally iconic scenes of rioters burning and looting the streets of Watts, Newark, Chicago, Baltimore, and numerous other cities during the same decade represent the destructive potential of behavior produced in large groups. In either case the resultant behavior bears the stamp of emergence; it is influenced by God. And as was the case with divine law, the influence of God in history can improve the state of affairs or degrade it. The mere fact that God's influence is present does not mean that the influence is a blessing. It is we who must decide whether God's intervention in history is a positive or negative one (though we now see how misleading the word "intervention" is, since it implies influence by a force outside of history, rather than a force that is part and parcel of history), and whether to embrace or reject it.

I realize that this understanding is disturbing to some. For a very long time, the prevailing belief has been that history deals out random hands of cards to us, and that when we get a really terrible hand, we may hope that God—the supernatural Fixer—will intervene at the last minute and patch things up. God will remove the disease, frustrate the attacking army, end the drought. But this model makes no sense anymore. Diseases, droughts, and earthquakes are not sent as retribution for sin; they are part of the natural world that we inhabit. And there is no supernatural Fixer who will magically swoop down at the very last moment to protect us, if we just pray hard enough and behave properly. There are, however, many parts of life (both good and bad) that are controlled or at least influenced by the emergent power of the interaction of huge numbers of human consciousnesses. These include starting wars and ending them, contributing to drought and minimizing its effects, fouling our environment and cleaning it up, abusing human beings and redeeming them from their abusers. The power reflected in these influences on life is immense. This is how I understand the claim that God intervenes. And this is, again, the way I understand the passage from Deuteronomy: "I call heaven and earth to witness against you today. I set before you life and death, blessing and curse. Choose life, that you and your descendants might live."[15] God does not just hand out goodies to the well behaved.

God, whether understood as the natural processes of disease or environmental conditions or as the emergent function of interacting human beings, hands out all sorts of things to all sorts of people. It's up to us to decide which parts of God's influence to welcome and embrace, and which parts to reject.

Impious as it may seem, the rejection of what God grants us is rooted deeply in our tradition. Much of traditional religious faith, including mainstream Jewish belief, teaches that God is responsible for death. Yet we also have an ancient tradition of fighting death, by doing things such as building secure houses for ourselves, ensuring that we have enough food, raising armies to protect ourselves against our enemies, and practicing medicine. Is a physician's fight to save a patient's life a rejection of God? In a way it is. But it is that very rejection that is our unique gift as beings who have the ability to make choices, to reject the "natural" course of things. It is, perhaps, a key difference between us and the rest of the animals.

To reject or fight against some of God's influences in life is not the same thing as denying that these negative influences are God's doing. Jewish tradition prefers us to acknowledge that certain negative forces in life are divine and reject them, rather than claim that only the good things in life are God's doing and that the rest is either the result of random chance or (the far worse option in the eyes of Jewish thought) that it reflects the influence of some malevolent Force opposed to God. This latter belief is dualism, and while there are not many things about which Jewish tradition speaks with a single voice, rejecting dualism is one of them. The very fact that Jewish tradition prescribes a blessing to be recited upon hearing tragic news demonstrates the degree to which God's influence is recognized in all events, both good and bad. God does intervene in—that is to say, influences—history. The difficult adjustment for many people is to understand that that simple statement is *not* code for "God makes everything all better, and when your world is falling apart, God can step in to fix things up." Eons of human experience have proven that this portrayal, enticing and appealing as it is, is more fantasy than reality.

A DIGRESSION: THE ANXIETY OF RESPONSIBILITY

I want to pause briefly to address a difficult issue that has lurked beneath the surface of much of the foregoing. Several times throughout these pages I have claimed that God acts in both positive and negative ways, and that it is the responsibility of each one of us to judge which aspects of divine activity to embrace, celebrate, and imitate, and which to reject and avoid. In Chapter Three I argued that God does command; that is, God does promulgate rules for human behavior. Some of them are good, moral, and just. Others are not. As with any set of rules, each individual must make a conscientious judgment about how to behave in relation to those rules. I now want to apply the same principle again. God has a will and does influence history. Sometimes God's will and influence drive humankind toward noble, caring behavior that we label with such terms as "holy," "sacred," or even "saintly." But sometimes God's will and influence drive us in exactly the opposite direction, to destroy, defile, and degrade one another and the world in which we live. Again, we must each judge when and how to accept divine influence as our guide and when and how to fight against it. The theme of personal responsibility keeps coming back, in different contexts but always with the same ultimate message: The burden of making good decisions rests squarely on my shoulders, and yours, and everyone else's. There is no easy way to avoid the burden, no secret guidebook or convenient litmus test to judge infallibly whether a particular action or decision or policy is Good or Evil, or even Neutral. Ethical life involves wrestling with such decisions and the wrestling is difficult, especially since long experience has taught us that no matter how hard we try, we sometimes make the wrong decisions and pay the price. It's important to acknowledge that this is a heavy load to bear.

It is also important to note, however, that Jews have always made such decisions. Since at least the dawn of the Talmudic era, Jewish thinkers and legal authorities have recognized the need to formulate interpretive principles to guide us in our observance of the laws of the Torah. In other words, although the Jews of antiquity believed absolutely that the Torah was God's revealed word, and although they believed that they were absolutely bound to obey God's word, they also realized that sometimes they would need to decide how—and even whether—to do so. In the terms of our present discussion, they needed to take responsibility for deciding when following the law was right or wrong. This claim may seem surprising in light of the common and widespread impression that the pious ones of ancient times, since they *really* believed that God had commanded them, would always follow the law unquestioningly, or at least feel guilty when they did not. But we need only consider one example, the well-known principle of *pikuach nefesh*, to recognize how mistaken such an impression is.

Generally translated as "saving a life," pikuach nefesh is a rabbinic principle requiring that almost every law of the Torah be violated if this be necessary in order to save a life. In the Talmud there are only three exceptions, three laws of the Torah that must *not* be broken even to save a life: murder, idolatry, and a whole category of biblically prohibited sexual offenses.[16] Outside these three, all other laws may—indeed must—be violated if doing so is required to save a life. This includes such prohibitions as working on the Sabbath, stealing, eating prohibited foods, and so on. These rules, according to the Talmud, are based on a couple of different biblical verses from the book of Leviticus. One says, "You shall not stand [idly] by the blood of your neighbor (Lev. 19:16)," which the rabbis interpret to mean that one is not to stand by and do nothing while another bleeds (that is, while another's life is in danger). Rather, one should act to save the life, even if the necessary action involves the violation of specific and serious biblical laws. The other verse says, "Therefore, you shall keep My statutes and My laws, which, if a person does them, he shall live by them (Lev. 18:5)." Here the rabbis interpret the words "live by them" as meaning "one should live by them, and not die by them."[17] Now while these interpretations sound completely rational and reasonable to the ears of most contemporary readers, it is important to point out that they *are* interpretations, and that they are *not* obvious conclusions to be drawn from the plain meaning of the biblical text. Neither of the cited verses explicitly counsels that the Torah's laws be violated in order to save a life. Rather, the rabbis have developed—or, to put it more starkly, have *invented*—an overarching principle and then used it to guide their interpretation so as to prove that the principle itself is found in the Torah.

It is true that for roughly the last two thousand years Jews have used their judgment in deciding how to interpret what they have taken to be divine law. And it is true that those interpretations have sometimes involved the effective suspension of biblical law. What is novel here is the idea that responsibility for making such decisions regarding interpretation lies with each individual. In premodern times there is little question but that the responsibility for such interpretation lay primarily with the Sages, the wise ones who were authorized (even though their authorization was often self-generated and jealously guarded) to make such major decisions. The three principles that generally function to strengthen the credibility of an interpretive innovation are that it be the work of a majority of Sages, that it date from antiquity, or that the interpreter(s) to whom it is originally attributed be of great preeminence. We have already seen the power of the majority in the Talmudic story of Aknai's oven, where the majority of the sages overrules the opinion of a single scholar. The issue of antiquity is based on the understanding that the closer (in time) a religious authority is to Moses and the original revelation at Sinai, the more he is to be trusted. And finally, any opinion attributed to a scholar of great renown is given far more weight than an opinion attributed to a lesser light of the rabbinic world.

These principles are quite reasonable and are shared by other legal systems. In American jurisprudence, for example, we look for opinions expressed by great scholars ("Professor So-and-So of the Yale Law School said that . . ."), or those endorsed by large groups ("The American Bar Association supports the notion that . . ."), or those attributed to earlier generations of scholars ("The great Supreme Court Justice Oliver Wendell Holmes often argued that . . ."; in this case we have both antiquity and preeminence), and these are all given great credence and respect. And there is some wisdom in privileging the positions of groups and preeminent individuals. In the former case it is assumed that a group's opinion will be crafted with more care, and will have to pass muster in a more rigorous evaluation process, than that of an individual. And in the latter case there is an assumption that if a particular individual is widely recognized as an outstanding expert in his or her field, then his or her opinion must be worth more than that of an average practitioner. The criterion of antiquity may function on either of two levels. An older opinion, simply because it is closer to ancient revelation or sacred sources and thus more likely to reflect original intent, may carry greater weight than a more recent opinion. Additionally, there may be a sense that any opinion that has been around for a very long time has had many opportunities to be discredited. If it remains respected despite such opportunities, it has withstood the test of time and should be held in high esteem. All in all, these shortcuts for deciding which interpretations of ancient tradition are right and which are wrong are reasonable and helpful.

But we now live in an age that remembers the Nuremburg Trials, where the world developed a new principle that trumps these traditional criteria. The new rule is that each of us is responsible for his or her own decisions. No matter how I arrive at my decisions,[18] at the end of the day I am the one who bears responsibility for my actions. Not God. Not my community, or my boss, or my commander. Just me. It certainly would be easier and more comfortable to make my decisions in a particular way because that's what the community expects me to do, or because that's what God has told me to do. It relieves me of the burden of making hard, personal choices. But once we come to see God as the natural emergent effect of interactions among ordinary people, relying blindly upon God or upon the rules of the community without evaluating their correctness is an irresponsible way to live one's life. There is certainly an element of loneliness and anxiety in living a life based primarily on personal responsibility, as anyone knows who has ever agonized over a personal decision for many hours or days. But the only alternative to this loneliness is the abdication of personal responsibility and the resultant collapse of any true sense of ethics. The ache of this fundamental ethical loneliness can be reduced somewhat by participation in community—a topic to which we shall return in due course.

THE MEANING OF PRAYER

Once we acknowledge that God is not a supernatural Being who chose to create the world, enter into covenantal relationships with us, give us instructions, and reward or punish us, the question of prayer must arise. For both traditional Jewish beliefs about prayer and the conclusions we reach by carefully reading traditional liturgical texts suggest that prayer only makes obvious sense in the context of a relatively traditional set of beliefs about God.

Once these beliefs change substantially, and the obvious rationale for prayer weakens or disappears altogether, we may take any one of a number of paths. We may decide that prayer is meaningless and simply choose not to pray. We may pray without thinking about the meaninglessness, thereby separating our intellectual convictions from our behavior and either ignoring or living with the tension. A variation on this option is to recite prayers occasionally, in times of trouble—personal crisis, illness, and so on—when people who are normally skeptical of the possibility of prayer's efficacy adopt the attitude of the punchline of the old joke, "It couldn't hurt!" Or we may engage in what I would call "worship activities," as distinct from prayer. That is to say, we may attend and participate in worship services as communal events that are steeped in tradition and filled with opportunities for social interaction, community building, and the reinforcement of group identity. Such events are meaningful and important per se, despite the fact that their apparent content (that is, the recitation of prayers of thanks and petition directed to God) conflicts with our modern, rational beliefs. Finally, we may restrict ourselves to finding meaning in the types of prayers that express our awe and wonder—our "radical amazement," to use Heschel's term—at the intricacy, the beauty, and the elegant structure of reality. These different options are not mutually exclusive. A rationalist is likely to engage in more than one of them at different times, depending on the circumstances of his or her life. But all of these options still leave me somewhat dissatisfied as I consider the core of Jewish prayer—statements made about, and requests addressed to, a sentient, aware, caring God. Consider the following examples, drawn from the heart of the daily liturgy:

> You have loved your people Israel with an eternal love. You have taught us Torah and commandments, laws and statutes. . . .
> You redeemed us from Egypt, Eternal our God, and delivered us from the house of enslavement. . . .
> Heal us, Eternal one, and we shall be healed; save us and we shall be saved. . . .
> Hear our voice, Eternal our God, pity us and be merciful to us. . . .
> Cause us to lie down in peace, Eternal our God, and to arise, our king, to life. . . .

These excerpts are completely typical of the tone of the daily liturgy. They express central tenets of the belief system(s) that frame Rabbinic Judaism:[19] God has a special, loving relationship specifically with the Jewish people. God gave the Jews a broad set of commandments, rules, and regulations. God brought the Israelites out of Egyptian slavery. God is the source of healing and can be appealed to for healing. God listens to prayer and protects and sustains individuals.

Is there a way to understand this system, and participate in it, rationally and meaningfully? Might the notion of God as the emergent result of the interconnectedness of and interactions among a huge number of consciousnesses make it easier for a Jew to recite the words of the traditional liturgy without either feeling hypocritical or somehow separating the prayer experience from one's beliefs? The answer is a resounding perhaps. Why such equivocation? Because some things are clear and others are not. It is clear to me that God's emergent consciousness does exist and that its existence is separate from our individual human existence. It is clear that as an emergent result of human interaction, God can have a special loving relationship with a particular group if that group develops, maintains, and celebrates its group identity.

It is also clear that an emergent God can and does legislate for human beings all the time, although (as we have seen) it is not possible to assume blindly that all such commandments are good and just. Rather, we must evaluate them and make judgments, just as we would with laws passed by any human legislature. It is clear that any social/political movement resulting in the redemption of a nation from its enslavement by another nation may well be regarded as an emergent process, and thus may well be seen as an "act of God." And finally it seems clear that human healing is more than a mechanical process, that in fact it is profoundly affected by human relationships, and that the caring of the community for one who is sick can make a significant difference in whether, how, and how quickly that person recovers. These observations would lead us to conclude that God does have some power to heal. This power, however, is not absolute, as we know from many instances where individuals succumb to illness despite the loving care bestowed upon them by a large community.

What is not at all clear is the nature and extent of awareness that an emergent God can have of individuals, and the nature and extent of awareness that an individual can have of the emergent God. To clarify this we must go back to the analogy between human neurons and human consciousness on the one hand, and conscious humans and God's consciousness on the other. I have argued that there is nothing more to the phenomenon of human consciousness than neurons, though those neurons must be immensely numerous and interconnected in a vast number of ways. Yet I cannot know—or be aware of—my individual neurons, except to know intellectually that they exist and that taken together they constitute what it means to be me. And an individual neuron in my brain cannot know me or even have the slightest inkling of the existence of the entity called Me. If the analogy I propose were perfect, we would have to conclude that God cannot know or be aware of an individual human being, and furthermore that an individual human being cannot know or be aware of God.

This is where my analogy becomes much less precise, however, since the very existence of religion and religious thought demonstrates that we *can* be aware of God's existence. And even if we cannot know what it is like to *be*

God (just as we cannot know what it is like to be a bat), we are nevertheless quite capable of asserting that God exists and even arguing about God's characteristics, powers, and limitations. I suggest that the imperfection in the analogy results from the enormous difference in complexity and sophistication between a single neuron and a single human self. While the neuron is undeniably an amazing piece of natural engineering and evolutionary creativity, an entire human self is incalculably more awesome in its structure, sophistication, and complexity. Perhaps human consciousness represents such a high level of emergence that it is the first emergence to be aware of the concept of emergence and of the existence of a higher-order emergence above its own level. After all, we humans are endowed with what appears to be a unique level of self-awareness, much higher and stronger than the levels of self-awareness that we observe even in the highest nonhuman mammals. Perhaps it is this self-awareness and depth of understanding that allows us to be aware of the existence of a level of emergence higher than our own, that which we call "God."

Given these observations about the uniqueness of our human level of emergent awareness, we might imagine that God—the emergent function of the interconnectedness of all our consciousnesses—is similarly able to know us. We might even argue that it is impossible to imagine that a consciousness arising as the emergent function of all interconnected human consciousnesses could be *less* aware than the individual consciousnesses that make it up. It might be only just as aware as they, but it is far more likely that it would be *more* conscious and aware than they are. It is fundamental to the nature of emergence, however, that the lower-level elements whose interconnectedness gives rise to the higher-level emergent phenomenon function according to different rules from those that govern the higher-level entity. This leads to a basic uncertainty at the heart of the notion of prayer. The structure and language of most prayers suggest that they are superficially similar to the kinds of statements we might make about, or to, other human beings. So, for example, the Yom Kippur liturgy has us say to God, "You know the secrets of the universe, and the hidden mysteries of all life." Viewed as ordinary language, this statement is not substantially different from what I might say to my friend, "You know how hard I studied for that test, you saw the hours I invested." The problem is that when I speak to my friend I am working with a basic assumption that his experience of life is roughly similar to mine. But if God is a higher-level emergent entity that functions with a completely different set of rules, I cannot make the same assumption. In fact, I have no idea whatsoever how God experiences existence.

The notion of my having a conversation with God quickly loses all of its meaning when viewed in the light of this insight. Of course there are workarounds by which I could still find meaning in the act of prayer. I could imagine my talking to God the way I think of talking to my dog, or talking to the ocean. In other words, I could simply benefit from expressing my thoughts, needs, and concerns in language. Almost everyone has at some point written a letter to another person without sending it. The very act of writing, of speaking one's mind, is useful. But that is not the real question. The real question is whether God *hears* prayer—that is to say, whether that higher-level emergent consciousness can be aware of, and understand, and care about *my* prayer. Given the model I have sketched out here, what meaning (if any) can there be in these words from the daily liturgy, the beginning of which I quoted above: "Hear our voice, Eternal our God, pity us and be merciful to us. And receive our prayer mercifully and willingly. For You are a God who hears prayers and supplications. Do not turn us away from before You empty[-handed], for You hear the prayer of Your people Israel in mercy. Blessed are You, Eternal, who hears prayer."

The answer is that I simply do not, and at least for now *cannot*, know. Can an emergent consciousness be aware of the specific states of each of its underlying components? If we pose the question by analogy—that is, by asking if I am (or can be) aware of the specific states of each of my neurons—then the answer seems to be no. But if each emergent phenomenon functions according to rules that are fundamentally different from the rules that govern its constituent parts, then it is risky to argue from the experience of the lower constituent parts to that of the emergent phenomenon. In other words, I am not aware of the states of each of my neurons (or of any of them), but the consciousness of God functions according to different rules from those that govern my experience.

This impenetrable veil blocking us from knowing what and how God knows may have one tiny peephole in it. If we assume that God's consciousness is the emergent result of the interconnectedness of all human consciousnesses, and we further assume that any action taken by any conscious human will somehow have an effect on the sum total of the emergent consciousness called God, then my act of prayer will have an effect on God. This claim is based on an idea called the butterfly effect, whereby even a very small change in a highly complex system will result in a change in the system as a whole. If the emergence of God's consciousness is susceptible to the butterfly effect (as I suspect it must be given its huge complexity), then my action, including my prayer, will have an effect on God. If we wish to define this as "hearing" or "being aware," then we may be able to conclude that in fact God is aware of my prayer.

But this is hardly a clear and comfortable resolution to the central prayer question. Complex systems that are characterized by sensitive dependence on initial conditions (the technical name for the butterfly effect) are so very complex that all we may say is that a tiny change in the system *may* result in a large, amplified change in the future state of the system. The phenomenon is called the "butterfly effect" because it is said that if a butterfly flaps its wings in Asia today, it may change the weather in North America next week. Applying that image to prayer, we can only say that my prayer may affect the future state of the system that is God's conscious self. But we cannot possibly say how it may affect the system, or when, or how much. So these observations, while they provide some small theoretical answer to the question of whether God hears prayer, in reality provide no religiously meaningful answer at all.

RETURN TO METAPHOR OR COMMIT TO UNCERTAINTY

In Chapter One I described how Professor Gary Kates challenged me as to whether I was still functioning exclusively in the realm of God-*metaphors* or if I had perhaps slipped inadvertently into thinking about God's actuality. The difference is significant. When we talk about metaphors, we are talking about suggestive images that do not name or describe a thing as it really is, but offer a useful (if imprecise) way of thinking about a thing. Metaphorical language is tremendously valuable, just as long as we do not forget that all metaphors are approximate, imprecise, and impressionistic, not precise or realistically descriptive.

Throughout the present chapter, and especially in the last section on prayer, it now seems as if we have only two choices. One possibility is to return to a self-consciously metaphorical way of thinking and speaking, whereby we constantly remind ourselves that the language of prayer is metaphorical language. It is not to be taken literally. When we talk about God hearing prayer, we do *not* mean that God hears prayer the way a parent hears a baby crying in the crib in the next room. When we say that God protects us, we do not mean that God protects us the way a Secret Service detail protects the president. These are suggestive, metaphorical habits of speech, meant to express some of the things we would like to believe about God. Our other option is to insist that the words mean what they say they mean, that they are *not* simply metaphors. But in that case we must accept a certain absolute limitation on our own knowledge. We cannot know what it is like to be God, nor can we know how God really functions. So we may make faith statements that begin with a Maimonidean "I believe with a perfect faith," but we must make them with a clear sense of our own absolutely limited knowledge. In either case the result is a significant degree of uncertainty in what we, as religious human beings, can truly know.

This degree of uncertainty leads to an important insight—namely, that in religious matters humility must be our primary attitude. We would be well advised to frame all expressions of belief in an attitude that says, "I believe this is so, but I am not really one hundred percent sure." Whether this hedge is expressed overtly or simply colors the background of our spiritual lives, it must always be present, for we can never really know for certain what it is like to be God. In addition to its being a philosophical necessity, this framework of humility offers the practical benefit of preventing (or at least attenuating) fundamentalism, triumphalism, and many of the intolerant abuses historically rooted in religion that have often given it such a bad name. If I cherish my beliefs deeply, but always remember that they include a small but inescapable element of uncertainty, I will be more inclined to listen to other human beings and may be more open to engaging with them in meaningful conversation. And any such conversations will evoke the presence of the emergent God.

NOTES

1. Gen. 1:26.
2. Gen. 2:18.
3. Gen. 6:6–7.
4. For an extended discussion of possible mechanisms for human free will, see Christof Koch, *Consciousness: Confessions of a Romantic Reductionist* (Cambridge, MA: MIT Press, 2012), chap. 7.
5. For highly comprehensible yet nontechnical explanations of quantum theory and the randomness associated with it, see my book *Judaism, Physics and God: Searching for Sacred Metaphors in a Post-Einstein World*, chap. 2. For more detailed and expert—but also nontechnical treatments—see Brian Greene, *The Elegant Universe* or Timothy Ferris, *The Whole Shebang: A State of the Universe(s) Report.*
6. A notable exception to this statement has led to many lively debates at our Seder table. The text in question is the repeated statement in Exodus that "God hardened Pharaoh's heart" just as the Egyptian monarch seemed ready to allow the Hebrews to leave. How could it be moral for God to make Pharaoh change his mind, leading to increased Egyptian suffering in the form of the plagues? This incident is the exception, not the rule, and reflects the fact that God, as portrayed in the Torah, is primarily interested in pursuing a covenant with Israel. What happens to other nations in the course of that process matters less. Pharaoh is used as a tool in God's ongoing effort to convince the Israelites to behave in a particular way. This explanation makes the text no less disturbing to me.
7. Deut. 30:19.
8. Pirkei Avot 3:19.
9. Babylonian Talmud, Berakhot 33b.
10. Babylonian Talmud, Shabbat 88a.
11. Maimonides, *Mishneh Torah*, Hilkhot Teshuvah, chap. 5.
12. From the traditional prayer book for the High Holidays. The translation is my own.
13. Pirkei Avot 2:4.
14. I place "echo" and "reverberates" in quotation marks to remind the reader that the Big Bang did not literally make a sound that could echo or reverberate, since there can be no sound in the vacuum of space. These words are meant to convey the sense that the very faint traces of energy left over from the Big Bang can still be detected in our universe today.
15. Deut. 30:19.
16. Babylonian Talmud, Sanhedrin 74a–b.
17. Babylonian Talmud, Yoma 85b, and elsewhere.
18. It is somewhat paradoxical that the more we know about human behavior, the more difficult it becomes to tease out of any individual human decision where it originated. Our thinking and judgment are profoundly influenced by the social contexts in which we are raised, educated, and live our lives. Nevertheless, the point here is that the final outcome of decision

making is one's own responsibility, even if the *process* of decision making is the product of a vast network of social factors.

19. Judaism certainly includes and represents many overlapping belief systems. But these statements seem to be at the common core of most, if not all, of them.

Chapter Six

The Ultimate Mitzvah

Here's a thought experiment: Get a large number of Jews together. Make sure they reflect a properly diverse Jewish population. There should be men and women, young Jews and old Jews, observant Jews and nonobservant Jews, Jews from different ethnic backgrounds and different geographical points of origin, Jews by birth and Jews by choice. They should all be thoughtful about Judaism. Then ask them the following question: what is the most important mitzvah in Judaism? The answers will be all over the map. Some will argue for Shabbat, others for kashrut, others for "Love your neighbor as yourself." Some will claim that the most important commandment is to remember that we were slaves in Egypt, while others will vote for "Remember what Amalek did." Some will take their cue from Emil Fackenheim and proclaim that "Thou shalt not grant posthumous victories to Hitler" is the most important, while others will suggest that supporting the State of Israel is the most important. Some will say, "Have Jewish babies!" and others will say, "Be a good person!" while others will cleverly go for "The study of Torah is equal to them all because it leads to them all."

If I were watching this thought experiment, I would be hard pressed to name my favorite. As each thoughtful respondent laid out his or her reasoning, I would nod in agreement, but then the next respondent would start to explain his or her position and again I would find it convincing. But in the end I would support none of their claims. My candidate for most important mitzvah would be in the very first instruction in the description of the experiment—that is, "Get a large number of Jews together." In other words, I would argue that the key to Jewish life is any mitzvah, any observance, any practice or activity that gathers people together in a community. For if God's consciousness is the emergent property of the interconnectedness among a large number of human consciousnesses, then whenever people gather,

God's presence is evoked, enlarged, and focused. Furthermore, the more interactive such an event is, the more powerful will be its capacity to evoke, enlarge, and focus the presence of God.

What kind of practices might serve to create this sort of divine emergence? Certainly the most obvious practice is prayer with a minyan, the quorum of ten Jewish adults that is the minimum required in order to hold a complete prayer service. Interestingly, there is no halakhic (i.e., legal) requirement to pray with a minyan, but it is strongly encouraged. Maimonides is very clear:

> The prayer of the community is always heard, and even if there were sinners among them [i.e., the minyan], the Holy One, blessed be He, never rejects the prayer of the multitude. Hence a person must join himself with the community, and should not pray by himself so long as he is able to pray with the community. And a person should always go to the synagogue morning and evening, for his prayer is only heard at all times in the synagogue. And whoever has a synagogue in his city and does not pray there with the community is called a bad neighbor.[1]

Two things are noteworthy about this text. First, for all the encouragement to pray with a minyan and all the warnings directed at those who have the opportunity to do so but choose not to, Maimonides does not use any language of legal prescription. This is a behavior that is praiseworthy and ought to be followed *if possible*. But if it is not possible, then the obligation to pray remains in effect and the individual is to pray alone. The second noteworthy aspect of this text is Maimonides's assertion that God always hears prayers uttered in a minyan, even if the group includes sinners. This claim, although perhaps surprising in the context of a more traditional understanding of God and prayer, makes perfect sense if we think of God as emergent. By definition, the gathering of ten (or more) individuals will evoke the divine presence. Note here that there is nothing magical about the number ten—either for emergence or, for that matter, for the minyan. It is an arbitrary number meant to convey a sense of community. It could be eleven or nine just as easily, though it could not be one or two. In fact, there is some evidence to suggest that in eighth century Palestine it was permitted to recite the entire service, including those sections that clearly require a minyan, with seven or even six people present.[2]

What is most curious is the fact that medieval law codes rule that if one member of the minyan falls asleep, he may still be counted.[3] In this particular case, because of the primacy of consciousness, I would argue that a sleeping person ought not be counted in a minyan, nor should one who is distracted (but more about distraction later). A ruling that is more in line with my views comes from a seventeenth century rabbi named Tzvi Ashkenazi, also known as the Chakham Tzvi. He wrote a *responsum* to the question of whether a golem could be counted in a minyan. A golem is a creature in the shape of a human, artificially created by the magical manipulation of Hebrew letters, especially of various forms and permutations of the names of God. The possibility of creating such a creature is first described in the Talmud[4] but its best-known form comes from traditions surrounding Rabbi Judah Loew, the Maharal of Prague (ca. 1520–1609). In this classic version, the rabbi creates a man-shaped creature out of mud, then inscribes the Hebrew word *emet* (truth) on its forehead, thereby bringing it to life. The creature then serves its maker, this service usually taking the form of protecting the Jews from attacks by non-Jewish marauders. Eventually, though, as the golem's strength grows, it begins to cause damage and harm to the Jews as well, and this leads the rabbi to return it to its original, nonliving state by erasing the *aleph* from the word emet on its forehead, leaving the word *met*, or "dead."

The question underlying the need for a responsum on whether such a creature may be counted in the minyan is whether it is truly alive and aware, or whether it is a sort of zombie, able to function physically but without mind or awareness. According to Gershom Scholem, some (but not all) medieval authorities believed that the golem has no "intellectual soul." Scholem notes the opinion of the sixteenth century Kabbalist Rabbi Moses Cordovero that "man has the power to give 'vitality' alone to the golem but not life [*nefesh*], spirit [*ru'ah*], or soul proper [*neshamah*]."[5] In modern terms, therefore, we may think of the golem as an animatronic robot Jew that, one might imagine, could stand, sit, walk around, put on a tallit, and even recite the words of prayer, but which we would probably not consider to be conscious and would probably not count toward a minyan.[6]

Since it seems that the very notion of community requires that the individual members of a group be conscious of the fact that there is a group and that they are intentional members of it, it makes sense to ask what level of consciousness a body must have in order to be considered a part of a minyan. Ten photographs or statues of Jews obviously would not constitute a minyan, nor—though I am uncomfortable even mentioning the possibility—would the bodies of ten dead Jews. But how about the bodies of ten comatose Jews? Would they constitute a minyan? If not (and I suspect most people would rule that way) then it is only a small step to say that ten sleeping Jews do not constitute a minyan, since a sleeping person is generally not aware of what is transpiring around him or her. These distinctions suggest that "conscious" is not a binary quality that either exists or does not exist, but rather describes a continuum. One who is sound asleep is hardly conscious at all (though, in neurological terms, such an individual is more conscious than one who is in a coma), while one who has just nodded off for a brief nap (as people sometimes do in synagogue) is far more conscious. If I had to decide whether a minyan was present, and we had nine wide-awake people and one person in a deep sleep, I would say we were short a tenth—whereas if we had ten wide-awake people and one of them nodded off, I would still be comfortable thinking that a minyan was present. By the same measure of consciousness (if we accept Cordovero's view), a golem likewise ought not count toward the required ten.[7]

BEYOND THE MERE MINYAN

All this being said, I would now argue that the minyan, the prayer quorum, is not the most effective Jewish setting in which to anticipate the presence of an emergent divine mind. The reason is that traditional Jewish prayer is not a very interactive activity. During some parts of the service, notably *Barchu* (the call to prayer), *Kedushah* (the sanctification of God in the Tefilah), and the *Kaddish*, when there are elements of call-and-response between the *shaliach tzibbur* (the person leading the prayers) and the congregation, there is some minimal interaction but it is completely scripted. And one might argue that during periods of congregational singing, there is also some minimal interaction among the members of the minyan, since singing in a group requires that one pay attention to the pitch, rhythm, and other characteristics of the song and try to match or harmonize with them. As a song sung communally gets faster or slower, or as the transition between a chorus and a verse or between a verse and a chorus occurs, the singers instinctively (I would even say "unconsciously," thereby making the situation more problematic) interact with one another. Similar minimal interaction may occur while a sermon is being delivered or while the Torah is being read. But by and large the synagogue service is not very interactive. Most of the attention of the worshippers is devoted to the proper recitation of the words of the *siddur* (prayer book), and perhaps to the personal and communal encounter with God that those words are meant to facilitate. Somewhat ironically, the height of interaction—that is, congregants chatting among themselves—although it occurs in some traditional congregations, is strongly discouraged in others. This is most notably the case in Reform congregations where there is an emphasis on proper decorum, and in many Orthodox congregations in Israel where there are placards posted saying "It is forbidden to converse during the time of prayer." With conversation discouraged, the prayer community (or minyan) is not best suited to result in the emergence of the divine presence, if that emergence depends on maximizing interpersonal interaction.

To find a better-suited communal gathering, we return to Maimonides's Laws of Prayer, in a section almost immediately following the excerpt quoted above: "The house of study [*beit hamidrash*] is greater than the synagogue. And the great sages, even though they had in their city many synagogues, would only pray in a place in which they engaged in [study of] Torah."[8] It is typical of Maimonides to give little background information to enable us to understand the thinking behind his rulings, but it is likely that in making this observation he is basing himself on the following statement in the Talmud (or one very similar to it): "Abaye said: At first I used to study at home and pray in the synagogue. But since I heard that Rabbi Hiyya bar Ammi said in the name of Ulla that since the day of the Temple's destruction the Holy Blessed One has nothing in the world but the four cubits of halakha, I only pray in a place that I study."[9] Here Abaye (an early fourth century Babylonian rabbi) gives us some insight into why he only prays in a place in which he studies the law. He relies on the tradition attributed to Hiyya bar Ammi in the name of Ulla, according to which God's "place" or location is in the four cubits—about six feet—of Jewish law. In its original context, this tradition implies that God's domain has shrunk in the aftermath of the destruction of the Temple in Jerusalem. While the Temple stood, it was believed that God dwelt in the Temple, which—at least in nostalgic memory—was seen as having been a tremendous and glorious building. When the building was destroyed by the Romans in 70 CE, God needed a new home and chose the four cubits of halakha.

The text raises several interesting questions, including how God could physically "reside" anywhere, the significance of the Temple and the effects on God of its destruction, and even the curious matter of how halakha can be measured in cubits (the cubit being a measurement of length). But what is quite clear from the text is that Abaye uses the phrase "the four cubits of halakha" as code for "the study of halakha." For if, as we may reasonably assume, his goal in prayer is somehow to encounter God, the fact that he chooses to pray only where he studies tells us that he believes that God's presence is associated with the act of study. But what is it about study that would attract the divine presence? A large part of the answer lies in the traditional Jewish preference for study in community—specifically, study in *chavruta*. Chavruta (also often spelled and pronounced *chevruta*) is an Aramaic word closely related to the Hebrew word *chaver*, or "friend." It describes a system in which students study in pairs, the two partners reading the text out loud and arguing over its meaning with the hope of arriving at a mutually agreed upon analysis. Although the method is most often associated with the old yeshiva world of Eastern Europe (and its descendants, the modern yeshiva worlds of Israel, North America, and elsewhere), in fact the value of study in partnership was recognized as early as the Talmud: "Form groups and engage in Torah [study] for the Torah is only acquired in *havurah* [i.e., the company of a group], for Rabbi Yosse ben Hanina said, '... [Those] who sit each one separately and study Torah ... become stupid.'"[10]

What is the advantage gained by studying with a partner or in a group? On a purely practical level, one may argue that group study is more effective because students feel an obligation to their partners or group members to show up and be prepared; it is harder to skip a session or prepare sloppily or half-heartedly when you know that others are depending on you. Furthermore, in the analysis of difficult concepts, different students may grasp ideas differently or may understand (and conversely, be confused by) different sections of a text. Bringing more minds to bear on a problem thus exploits the individual strengths of each student and compensates for the weaknesses of each. And often we are not really sure we have understood a concept until we have tried to explain it to, or discuss it with, others. But I would suggest that the importance of chavruta study goes far beyond its practical value, for Torah study—and particularly Torah study in chavruta—is arguably the most efficacious way to encounter God.

This notion seems to have been an innovation of the Talmudic era. Nowhere in the Bible do we get a sense that study was an important part of ancient Israelite life. But in the first few centuries of the Common Era, perhaps under the influence of the Hellenistic emphasis on reason and the search for truth, the evolving system of Rabbinic Judaism defined study as the most important sacred activity. In a Talmudic passage that is included in the opening pages of the daily morning service, a list is proposed of things "for which a person receives the 'interest' in this world, while the 'principal' is stored for the world to come." The list includes honoring one's parents, dowering poor brides, caring for the dead, and even promoting peace among human beings. But it concludes with "The study of Torah is equivalent to all of them."[11] But why should this be so? It seems that in the period of evolution from the biblical to the rabbinic era, a shift occurred in the Jewish perception of how God was to be encountered. In ancient times, at least according to the received sacred memories, the encounter was mediated by the *kohanim* (the priests) who presided over the sacrificial rites of the Temple. The interaction was direct and mysterious. It reached its peak on the afternoon of Yom Kippur when the High Priest would enter the very heart of the Temple complex, the Holy of Holies, and pronounce the four letter personal name of God, while in the outer court the people all fell prostrate.

But in the period following the Temple's destruction, the Jewish world saw the growth of a new idea. Encounter with God would no longer be—perhaps *could* no longer be, because the Temple no longer existed—nearly so direct. The rabbis were distinctly aware that God was not "talking" to them any more as He had in the days of the prophets. Instead God was to be sought, and ultimately found, only in the Torah—the divine but highly encrypted message that God had left for the people. The Torah was, and is, all that is left of God's palpable presence. Engaging with it becomes the most important way to interact with God. But "engaging with it" does not mean reciting its words or committing them to memory, as is the case in some other faith traditions. For Judaism "to engage" the text is to discuss it, analyze it, or, in the words of a rabbi identified as Ben Bag-Bag, "Turn it and turn it, for everything is in it."[12] In fact, the more we look at the rabbis' attitudes toward

Torah study, the more it seems that it was the act of study per se, and not the object of study (i.e., the Torah), that was most important to them. It is in the very act of students gathering together to discuss, dissect, and argue over the meaning of text that we find God. It is not much of an exaggeration to say that it does not even matter what the topic is. What matters is the intellectual encounter, the formation of a community of engaged minds.

The strength of this rabbinic belief can be seen in a brief rabbinic comment on the rather harsh biblical law of the "stubborn and rebellious son." According to Deuteronomy 21:18–21, if a man has a stubborn and rebellious son, the son is to be brought to the elders of the town and stoned to death. An early anonymous comment on this law says, "There never was a stubborn and rebellious son, and there never will be. So why was it written? To teach 'Interpret it and receive a reward.'"[13] In other words, according to the author of this text, the biblical law had no practical value but was included in the Torah to provide an opportunity for study and interpretation of the Torah and the reward attendant thereto. When Jews engage in study, God is met in the community—or, to use the language that I have proposed, God's presence emerges.

SYNAGOGUE AND STUDY HOUSE WITHOUT RELIGION

If the ultimate mitzvah is the formation of community, it is clear that, historically speaking, the two primary expressions of the mitzvah were prayer in a minyan and text study in chavruta. But we now live in an era in which most Jews are *not* religiously observant. In their personal lives, they behave in most respects like their Gentile neighbors, and they certainly do not often (for many of them the more accurate word is "ever") spend time in synagogues or study houses. But this shift away from the two classical expressions of the ultimate mitzvah should not mislead us into thinking that God cannot or does not emerge in their midst. In the early twentieth century, Rabbi Abraham Isaac Kook—known by all as Rav ("Rabbi") Kook and often considered the father of Religious National Zionism—declared that the secular, nonreligious Zionists in Palestine, despite their self-conscious and deliberate rejection of religion, were nevertheless tied to God: "Jewish secular nationalism is a form of self-delusion: the spirit of Israel is so closely linked to the spirit of God that a Jewish nationalist, no matter how secularist his intention may be, must, despite himself, affirm the divine. An individual can sever the tie that binds him to life eternal, but the House of Israel as a whole cannot."[14]

Here Rav Kook is claiming that even though the secular Zionists *claimed* and *intended* to be nonreligious (or even antireligious), the way they lived their lives, creating Jewish communities to build up the Jewish land, was a testimony to God's presence. A more recent and even broader expression of the idea is found in the work of Rabbi Irving Greenberg, an American Orthodox leader who in the late 1970s began to speak about "holy secularity." Greenberg claims that the conditions of modernity in general, and the impact of the Holocaust in particular, have shifted the locus of holiness from the synagogue and the yeshiva to a much broader range of secular loci of community. His professional life in the 1980s and 1990s focused on such places as the Jewish federation, the Jewish community center, and the various non-religious Jewish organizations dedicated to *tikkun olan* (literally, repairing the world; that is, engaging in social justice) as places where God's presence can be felt.[15]

Indeed, these claims make perfect sense in the context of the notion of God's consciousness as the emergent property of interacting human consciousnesses. I will take Kook and Greenberg a logical step further, however, and claim that God's emergence is in no way limited to Jewish interactions. In any place or situation in which human consciousnesses interact, God's presence emerges and the more intense and intentional the interaction, the more powerful the emergence. Thus, in a college or university classroom where students and faculty engage one another over ideas, God's presence emerges. But the lecture hall, where a single professor at the front of the room lectures and projects Power Point slides as a hundred students sit watching and listening (or perhaps not) in silence, will be a less propitious environment for such emergence to occur than the seminar room in which a dozen students and their professor argue about the meaning of a passage in Plato, or the impact of global free trade agreements on local economies, or the significance of race in Shakespeare.

In an attempt to inculcate a greater sense of community and connectedness among my students at Bard College, I now open every class session with a five- or ten-minute period of chavruta study. I distribute copies of a brief text— something relevant to that day's topic, a paragraph or two—and ask my students to pair up. I remind them to make sure they know their partner's name, then to read the text out loud to one another and discuss it. I began this practice out of a concern that there was not a strong enough sense of community in the classroom, but after a couple of semesters' worth of experience, I have heard from numerous students that the chavruta study is their favorite part of the class. Even though most of my teaching takes the form of facilitated discussion rather than lecture, many students still feel uncomfortable speaking up and being heard in a group of twenty, whereas when discussing a text with just one study partner they have no choice but to speak and to listen. And although I would never present this process in a secular and mostly non-Jewish academic setting as a way of evoking God's presence, the sense of community that my students report seems to me to do exactly that.

Beyond the classroom and even beyond the context of formal education, similar examples of interaction leading to emergence can be found throughout our society, again without invoking anything that looks like traditional religion or religious practice. Team sports, political activities, and cultural events could all be seen as venues for interaction and emergence, though again I would qualify the observation by noting that the more intentional the interaction, the more profound will be the emergence. In short, the presence of God is proportional to the quantity, intensity, and deliberateness of the interaction, no matter what the topic or who the participants may be. And here I will borrow the claim made by Rav Kook in the above-cited quotation: even when the participants in the interaction think they are nonreligious, and even when their intentional stance is opposed to religion (as is often the case in a liberal arts college like Bard), the interactions of which they are a part cannot help but create an emergent higher-level consciousness—the consciousness of God.

EMERGENCE AND THE CHOSEN PEOPLE

The claim made in the previous paragraph raises an important Jewish question: if God's mind, God's consciousness, is the emergent property of the massive interconnectedness of human consciousnesses, and if that interconnectedness can happen in any venue and among any group of conscious humans (or other conscious creatures, for that matter), what makes God's covenant particularly or uniquely Jewish? What is the meaning of the blessing recited before the reading of the Torah that identifies God as the One "who chose us from among all peoples and gave us His Torah"? My answer here is no different from the answer I have often given with regard to the Creator stage of God, that set of natural laws that produced the structured, elegant universe in which we find ourselves. Neither that stage of God, nor the emergent, conscious stage of God, which humans have been aware of for thousands of years, is in any way attached more to any one group than to any other. The parochial elements of any particular religion—be they sacred texts, laws, worship practices, or other behaviors or traditions—are the product of the interconnectedness of the members of that particular group. So the Torah and all of the Jewish laws, narratives, values, and practices that flow from it are, as I explained earlier, the product of Jewish community, Jewish interaction. Other faiths' sacred texts and traditions, all legitimately revealed by God, are likewise the product of those faiths' communities. This does not imply by any means that there are multiple Gods. Rather, each group, each community experiences God in its own manner. Such diversity in the experience of the divine is well known even to ancient Jewish tradition. Consider the following midrash:

"I am the Eternal your God . . . ." Why is this said? Because God appeared at the [Red] Sea as a hero doing battle, as it is written, "The Eternal is a man of war . . ." (Ex. 15:3), but God appeared at Mount Sinai as an elder, full of mercy, as it is written, "And they saw the God of Israel . . ." (Ex. 24:10). And when they were redeemed, what does it say? "[. . . Under His feet there was the likeness of a pavement of sapphires,] like the very sky for purity . . ." (Ex. 24:10). And it also says, "As I looked on, thrones were set in place [and the Ancient of Days took His seat. And the hair of His head was like lamb's wool. His throne was tongues of flame; its wheels were blazing fire.] A river of fire streamed forth before Him . . ." (Dan. 7:9–10). In order not to give the nations of the world any basis to say, "There are two Powers" [Scripture said], "I am the Eternal your God,"—it was I in Egypt, it was I at the Sea, it was I at Sinai, it was I in the past, it [will be] I in the future to come.[16]

The logic of this rather early rabbinic text is no different from that which I am proposing: God appears at different times and in different circumstances and different ways, but this should not lead us to imagine that these different manifestations of God represent different Gods. To this ancient argument, I am simply adding the notion that God appears differently to different human communities—Jews, Muslims, Christians, Buddhists, Hindus, and so on. The only respect in which this notion diverges from a more traditional view is that many religious groups throughout human history, including Jews, have claimed that the Truth of their God (or at least their *experience* of God) invalidates the claims of any other groups to different experiences of God. In the context of this belief, it is perfectly legitimate for Jews or any other group to claim that their experience of God makes them feel as if their group is chosen and special. The critical caveat is that any such claim should be made with the awareness that other groups' experiences of God having chosen *them* are no less legitimate or worthy of respect.

TECHNOLOGICAL CONNECTEDNESS

There are two assumptions underlying much of what I have written in these pages that I want to focus on here. First of all, consciousness is a good and valuable thing. More consciousness is better than less consciousness. A universe with consciousness is better than a universe without consciousness. For me these beliefs are axiomatic; they need no justification, no proof. They are most likely the result of a conceit that is hardwired into us as quintessentially conscious creatures. Second, consciousness results from interconnectedness. Individual consciousness results from the huge interconnectedness that characterizes the brain, billions and billions of neurons interconnected in trillions and trillions of ways. The more interconnectedness, the more consciousness. Likewise, group consciousness results from the interconnectedness of group members. The more they are interconnected, the more conscious the group becomes. And finally, as I have argued, God's consciousness is the emergent result of the interconnectedness of all other consciousnesses.

This being said, it is easy to be uncritically thrilled with the technologies that seem to have increased human interconnectedness throughout our history as a species. The beginning of this process came in the evolution of spoken language, which allowed for deeper, more abstract, and more sophisticated interaction among our ancestors. This crucial development is thought to have occurred at the very dawn of our species, though there is no way to determine with any precision when language first appeared. By 3000 BCE written language had been developed. This permitted people to communicate and connect with those in other places and other times, whereas verbal communication had limited us to communication with those in our immediate surroundings. In the fifteenth century, the printing press was invented. The telegraph was invented in the 1830s, followed some forty years later by the telephone and by radio in the 1890s. In the twentieth century, the quality of all these technologies increased as the cost decreased and a larger and larger portion of the world's population made use of them. New technologies (television, word processing, the fax machine) were added, and all of them helped increase the scope and depth of human interconnection. The crowning glory of the process (at least so far) was the personal computer and its descendants—the tablet, the smartphone, and all the other wired and wireless devices with which we now communicate effortlessly and cheaply over immense distances.

At each stage in this process, it has become easier for more human beings to connect with other human beings. The increase in the number of people communicating, and the complexity of the networks of communication facilitated by the growth of technologies, has had—and will continue to have—a profound impact not only on the life of human beings but, in the context of viewing God as emergent, in the life of God as well. Think about it. In the fourteenth century, it would take many months for a scribe to copy the text of the Torah with commentary. After all that effort, only one copy would be produced that would consequently be enormously expensive. A few scholars could sit around a table in a study house and read it together, but the extent of its influence would have been limited. How things have changed! On July 18, 2013 I searched on Amazon.com for a similar book—that is, the Torah with commentaries. I found several, including *The Commentator's Bible-Numbers: JPS Miqra'ot Gedolot* for $53.06. If I wanted it the next day, I would just have had to specify "one day shipping" and pay a bit more. And by the way, this book on that day was ranked in Amazon's best-sellers rank at #107,462 out of a total inventory of somewhere between 1.8 million and 5 million titles.

These mind-boggling figures demonstrate that the amount of interconnectedness in the world today is vastly greater than was the case seven centuries ago, and even seven decades ago. And the rate of change seems to be increasing steadily. Since the beginning of the twenty-first century, our connectedness has mushroomed with the invention and growth of social media. Facebook, Twitter, Instagram, Pinterest, Tumblr, Yik Yak, YouTube, SMS, Instant Messaging, and a host of other Internet-based communications modalities have created a sense that we can be in touch with everyone we know, and even with people whom we do not know, at all times. If I buy *The Commentator's Bible* that I used as an example above, I can start a Facebook group (or a Google group or a Yahoo group) of people interested in reading and discussing it. I can blog about it and set up my blog to encourage comments. I can study with dozens or hundreds of people whom I have never met. As long as they share a common language with me and have a computer (or a smart phone or other digital communication device), we can establish a virtual beit midrash. In short, in today's world more people are more closely in touch with more people, and are engaged with them over more ideas, than has ever before been the case in our planet's history. We humans are vastly more interconnected than ever and that means that God is vastly more conscious. It seems that God's presence is growing more palpable at a breathtaking, dizzying rate.

THE DOWNSIDE OF TECHNOLOGY

All interconnections among people are not created equal. I argued above, for example, that the interconnectedness of a minyan at prayer is somehow "less" than that of students discussing text in chavruta in a beit midrash, and that the interconnectedness of several hundred students sitting passively in a lecture hall is somehow "less" than that of a dozen students sitting with their professor around a seminar table. I have put the word "less" in quotation marks to indicate that it is not entirely clear exactly how one sort of connectedness is less than another. Perhaps a mathematician might be able to analyze and actually quantify connectedness, whether of people or computers or neurons, but such quantitative calculations are not as important to me as the essential quality of the interconnectedness. The latter can be determined by intuitive analysis of any particular situation. My many years of experience in classrooms convinces me that there is less interaction going on in a lecture hall than in a seminar. If I lecture to fifty people and all are paying attention, there are fifty different connections being made. If during the lecture five students ask questions, then we can add five more connections. But if I sit around a seminar table with ten students and they are all really engaged in the discussion, each one of us can connect to every other one and with subgroups, so that the number of connections quickly grows very large. The point is that simply putting people in a room together does not necessarily create a community of interconnectedness, nor are any two given collections of people necessarily of equal connectedness.

Let us apply this simple observation to the world of digital connectedness, the world of smart phones, Facebook, text messages, and all the many related technologies that currently dominate our culture. Earlier I wrote, "We humans are vastly more interconnected than ever and that means that God is vastly more conscious. It seems that God's presence is growing more palpable at a breathtaking, dizzying rate." But when we examine our electronic interconnectedness more critically, it turns out not to be exactly what it seems. Sherry Turkle is a professor at MIT and founder and director of the MIT Initiative on Technology and Self. Her 2011 book *Alone Together: Why We Expect More from Technology and Less from Each Other* contains some sobering caveats about the digitally interconnected world. Several of her points raise questions about the negative effect of connectedness on connectedness, paradoxical as that may sound.

Let's start with my observation that simply putting people in a room together does not necessarily create an interconnected community. In considering the widespread contemporary phenomenon of people being together in a space outfitted with WiFi (for example, a cafe), Turkle writes, "A 'place' used to comprise a physical space and the people within it. What is a place if those who are physically present have their attention on the absent? At a cafe a block from my home, almost everyone is on a computer or smartphone as they drink their coffee."[17] This common phenomenon has changed the meaning of human gatherings.

In his 1989 book *The Great Good Place*, sociologist Ray Oldenberg described the importance in society of what he called the "third place." One's "first place" is one's home and one's "second place" is one's workplace. But the third place is a neutral public space where people congregate informally and where community is created, strengthened, and nurtured. Traditional third places include parks and town squares, cafes and pubs, barber shops and beauty salons, and so on. Every society, Oldenberg claims, needs such places. Now, however, it seems that one can (and many do) sit in a third place without really being there, because one is focused on people or things that are elsewhere. The result is that the very cultural venues that have been developed to connect us to one another lose their ability to do so, because the individuals who come to such places carry with them an easy means to focus on—essentially to *be*—elsewhere. What initially appears to facilitate an increase in connectedness ends up, because of technological connectedness, disconnecting us from one another.

This paradox reminds me of an individual with whom I once worked. Whenever I was in his office, whether we were just chatting casually or discussing some serious matter, if his phone rang, he would immediately pick it up. This habit, which struck me as somewhat strange at the time, has now become commonplace. We have all had the experience of having a conversation with someone only to have that person's cellphone ring or vibrate and seeing him or her interrupt the conversation to take the call or answer the text. The clear message is: no matter how important my conversation with *you* is, the person calling or texting me *might* be more important, so I will always interrupt my conversation in the here and now to take this call or read and reply to this text. I have come to see this behavior as a violation of a Jewish principle. In numerous places in the Talmud we read that "*ha-osek ba-mitzvah patur min ha-mitzvah* [one who is engaged in a mitzvah is exempt from a mitzvah]." This means that if I am in the middle of fulfilling an obligation, I need not interrupt my performance of that obligation in order to fulfill a different obligation. So, for example, the halakha clearly states that a person whose close relative has died but has not yet been buried is exempt from all positive commandments (for example, prayer, putting on tallit and tefillin, etc.). One explanation for this law is that it is assumed that from the moment a person dies until the moment of burial, the immediate relatives of the deceased are engaged in the mitzvah of burying the dead. Even though the mitzvah of caring for and burying the dead obviously does not entail tasks at every moment between the time of death and the moment of burial, the law assumes that during that entire time the family members are engaged (at least psychologically or emotionally) in that mitzvah. Therefore they need not interrupt their performance of it to fulfill a different mitzvah. I apply this same principle to the mitzvah of speaking with another human being. When I am speaking with my friend, that interaction is a sacred moment (an obligation, if you will) because of its recognition of my fellow human being as a fellow image of God. The holiness of the act of conversing becomes even more profound in light of my proposal regarding the emergent nature of God. Any conversation is a mitzvah because it is part of the process of interaction in which God's presence emerges. Thus, according to the Talmudic principle, while I am engaged in the mitzvah of speaking with one person, I need not interrupt—a stronger position would be that I *ought* not interrupt—to engage in a different conversation.

Another instance of high-tech communications actually causing an impoverishment of real interconnectedness comes in the fact that young people, those sometimes known as "digital natives,"[18] generally avoid using the telephone to communicate, preferring to text one another. Turkle quotes Mandy, a high school sophomore whom she interviewed:

"You wouldn't want to call because then you would have to get into a conversation." And conversation, "Well, that's something where you only want to have them when you want to have them." For Mandy, this would be "almost never. . . . It is almost always too prying, it takes too long and it is impossible to say 'good-bye.'" ... Awkward good-byes feel too much like rejection. With texting, she says, "you just ask a question and then it's over."[19]

Turkle's many informants seem to agree that communications technology can be a useful tool to avoid real communication. Face-to-face interactions and even phone calls are too personal, too prying, too intimate. Communication via text message (or email, for the older generation) is scrubbed clean of intimacy and real feelings, replacing them with a broad palette of grinning, winking, grimacing, pouting, weeping, and laughing emoticons.

Avoiding the telephone is not the only way that communications technology facilitates avoidance of real interactions. Turkle devotes a whole section of her book to confession sites. These are Internet sites on which people can post confessions of their misdeeds and "unload" all of the secrets and shameful admissions that weigh them down. The confessions are made anonymously and the sites are set up so that people can comment on a confession. The problem with these online confessionals, says Turkle, is that they "do not lead [the users] to talk to those [they have] wronged or to try to make amends. [They go] online to feel better, not to make things right." Again, in the name of greater connectivity through digital technology, people end up avoiding real interactions with others.[20]

Even if we admit that communications technology sometimes—or often—is used to escape real, personal interaction, there are many ways in which people actually connect technologically. Social media platforms and online games and simulations are used by millions of people. Many of these people claim to have close, deep, meaningful relationships in these online worlds. But here too Turkle points to problems:

> When I speak of a new state of the self, itself, I use the word "itself" with purpose. It captures, although with some hyperbole, my concern that the connected life encourages us to treat those we meet online in something of the same way we treat objects—with dispatch. It happens naturally: when you are besieged by thousands of e-mails, texts and messages—more than you can respond to—demands become depersonalized. Similarly, when we Tweet or write to hundreds or thousands of Facebook friends as a group, we treat individuals as a unit. ... With sociable robots, we imagine objects as people. Online, we invent ways of being with people that turns them into something close to objects.[21]

I first became aware of the concerns that Turkle is expressing here some years ago, when I began to hear about Facebook. As I spoke with more and more people who used Facebook, mostly undergraduates and young adults in their twenties, I began to feel uncomfortable with the term "friend" as it is used on Facebook. There are strong connections between the language we use and how we think about the world. When Facebook appropriated the very old word "friend" and repurposed it as a label for individuals who are on my list of Facebook contacts, it seemed as if more and more young people who use Facebook were making less and less of a distinction between Facebook friends and "real" friends. According to a 2011 study put out by the Pew Internet and American Life Project, American users of Facebook at the time of the study had an average of 229 friends each and, again on average, had never met 7% of their Facebook friends.[22] But if we look not at all Facebook users, but only at younger ones, the figures shift dramatically. According to a 2011 article in the British press, the average 22-year-old in Britain had over a thousand friends.[23]

Two things strike me about these figures. First of all, no one has more than a thousand "real" friends. Rock stars, authors, actors, or politicians may have that many fans, or more, but no one has that many friends, if we define a friend in the traditional, pre-Facebook sense. So the idea that young people might have over a thousand Facebook friends, or even half of that number, raises troubling questions about the use—in fact, the *mis*use—of the word "friend." Second, the fact that the average Facebook user in the Pew study had never met 7% of his or her Facebook friends lends an air of absurdity to the use of the word. In fact, what has happened in this situation is that the essential meaning of the word "friend" has been changed. A friend is no longer someone I care about and who cares about me, whom I can count on for assistance and sympathy in times of trouble and who can count on me, in whom I can confide and who can confide in me. The concept has been emptied of all its meaning and is now used to connote a vague and often impersonal relationship. If we are not convinced that this is so, an additional detail that may sway us is the idea that, on Facebook, one can *un*friend a person as easily as one can friend him. And even if a Facebook user tells me that he or she obviously understands the difference between real friends and Facebook friends, I put too much stock in the relationship between thought and language to be completely convinced. Rather, I believe that this is an instance of the subtle degradation of the very notion of intimate, personal, deep relationships. Again, the technological paradox confronts us squarely: a revolutionary development in human culture that is hailed and celebrated as a way to increase and deepen human connectedness (and therefore, by my reasoning, the emergence of God) has the opposite effect. It makes such connectedness less intimate, less deep, less significant. As such, it must also diminish the emergent divine self.

The premise of this chapter has been that the creation of community is the ultimate mitzvah. On this sacred notion, I give Turkle the last word: "Communities are constituted by physical proximity, shared concerns, real consequences, and common responsibilities. Its [*sic*] members help each other in the most practical ways.... What do we owe to each other in simulation? ...

What real-life responsibilities do we have for those we meet in games? Am I my avatar's keeper?"[24]

CREATING COMMUNITY IN THE DIGITAL AGE

Creating community is the ultimate mitzvah. The minyan is one traditional setting in which to fulfill it, although, as we have seen, the beit midrash is even better suited to the task. We now ask how these traditional activities might be affected by the overwhelming presence of digital, mobile, computerized communication in today's world. In Maimonides's description of the minyan, we find the following: "And all these things [i.e, all parts of the service that may only be done with a minyan] if they were started in [the presence of ten] and some of them left (even though they should not have done so), the rest may finish. And all of them must be in one place, with the shaliach tzibbur [the one leading the prayers] with them in the same place."[25]

This passage makes it quite clear that those who constitute the minyan, the ten, must be in the same place. But the concept of "place" has changed in our day. When we use the Internet, we use the language of place. We talk about "going into a chat room" or "visiting a website." We know of websites that are "web portals" and we have been on sites that have a clickable button labeled "Enter." These uses of language cannot help but affect our sense of what place is, how one place relates to another, and what it means to be in a place or to not be in a place. In a related development, broadband Internet connections and webcams have led to the development of such services as Skype, Facetime, and many others whereby people can converse via video chat, often for free. The impact of these services, at least according to the fond hopes of their developers, is that people from all over the world will be able to "meet face to face" without getting on a plane and spending time and money traveling to be together physically. In such a cultural environment, we must eventually ask, as some already have, about the feasibility of a Jewish community—a synagogue, a minyan, or a beit midrash—that exists completely online. But before we jump to considering that radical possibility, let's approach it by degrees.

Several times I have attended Biennial Conventions of the Union for Reform Judaism. These events have typically attracted about 5,000 individuals from Reform congregations throughout North America and beyond. They are held in large convention centers and Shabbat services are enormous. Those conducting the service are on a platform way up at the front of the immense hall, and it's difficult or impossible to see or hear them from the back. But the problem is solved technologically by having a Jumbotron, an enormous television screen (or several such screens) positioned throughout the hall so that the congregation can see the shlichei tzibbur (service leaders) up close. Essentially, this is no different from giving everyone binoculars so they can see what's happening from a distance. As long as one is comfortable with the use of electronic equipment on Shabbat (something that would disturb a more traditionally observant population but that is generally acceptable in the Reform Jewish world), it's hard to imagine an objection to this system. Now if it is acceptable to sit in the last row of a 5,000-member congregation and watch the shaliach tzibbur on a large screen, what difference would it make if, instead of being inside the hall, we were to step out into the lobby and find another huge screen out there that allowed us that up-close-and-personal view of the rabbi and the cantor? Most people, I think, would still regard that as being there. But now let us imagine that this convention center is so sophisticated that it allows what happens in the main event hall to be broadcast to the televisions in the guest rooms of the five largest and closest hotels. Now I don't even have to show up for the service in order to be there, at least virtually. The problem is that this slippery slope argument that takes a participant farther and farther from a communal experience seems to ignore the ineffable power of actually being with other people. There is, in fact, something essentially different about being *with* a group of people in the same physical space that the group occupies and being virtually connected with that group by video hookup, no matter how large the display, how clear the resolution, and how life-like the audio. I can only speculate about what this essential difference is all about. Perhaps it is related to the human need for physical contact. Or perhaps there are tiny, subtle communicative signals that are exchanged among people when they are in close physical proximity to one another that simply cannot be detected or transmitted by audio and video devices. Whatever the case may be, there is clearly a difference between the experience of intimacy in the same physical space—be it with one other person, nine others, or a hundred others—and watching and listening to that experience on a television or computer screen. For this reason I would argue that a virtual minyan, in which all ten (or more) members are there by virtue of a web-based computer connection, is at best a pale and feeble substitute for actually being with the community. At its worst, given the growing habit of multitasking, worshippers in a virtual minyan could, while participating, also check email and Facebook, play games, watch YouTube videos, and so on. Most observers, I think, would regard such divided attention as a critical obstacle to *kavannah* (intention, focus) in prayer if it occurred in the synagogue, so how much the more so in the virtual synagogue.

There is, in fact, at least one online-only synagogue already in existence. It is called OneShul and its website includes the following message: "Please note that at this time, we do not do weddings, conversions to Judaism or other 'in person' Jewish rituals."[26] I am somewhat perplexed by the clearly implied recognition in this statement that some Jewish rituals can only be done "in person," at least "at this time," though the owners of the site seem to have left open the possibility that at some future time even these rituals will be possible online. Other rituals (including, according to the OneShul website, regular Shabbat and Holiday services and classes) can take place "virtually." In a 2012 online article about OneShul, its cofounder Michael Sabani wrote, "Our computers act as doorways, giving us access to the live sight and sound of the service leader. As long as everyone can hear the leader and participate, there really is no reason why all who are watching and participating can't be counted in a service minyan."[27] With all due respect to—and admiration for—the spirit of technological experimentation and innovation expressed in this statement, I would suggest that at best our computers are windows that allow us to watch, not doorways that allow us to enter, and that there is more to being part of a community than being able to see and hear the live sight and sound of it. I do not know whether that "more" has to do with subtle olfactory cues, or subconscious tactile cues, or some other human communicative modality so delicate that we are not consciously aware of it. But I know that there *is* a difference between being with people and seeing and hearing them via computer or television screen. And this difference, whatever its essential character, lends a level of depth, intimacy, and authenticity to an in-person meeting that simply does not come across in the digitally transmitted sight and sound. And I do not believe that anyone who has ever hugged a mourner after a minyan at a shiva house, or danced around the synagogue with a bride and groom at an *aufruf* (the celebratory acknowledgement of an upcoming wedding, usually held on the Sabbath preceding the wedding), can honestly claim otherwise.

This is not to say that there is no value in the electronic communication on which we have become increasingly dependent year by year. In a complex society in which people have multiple, varied commitments to work, community affairs, social life, and more, greater efficiency in communication can be of tremendous benefit to community. Here's an example: In the 1980s and 1990s, I lived in a tight-knit Jewish community in Teaneck, New Jersey. It would occasionally happen that participants at the weekday evening service at our synagogue would find themselves one or two people short of a minyan. Often members of the group were there because they were saying Kaddish (the memorial prayer for the dead, traditionally recited daily during the eleven months following the death of a close family member) and they could not fulfill this obligation without at least ten people present. So with services scheduled to begin at 8:00 pm, by 8:05 or 8:10 someone would go down the hall to the synagogue office, pick up a phone, and start calling people who lived close by. Several times I received such calls: "Hi David. We're at *shul* and we need a couple of more people for a minyan. Can you come over?" I am certain that, by now, the minyan coordinator takes out a smartphone and sends a text blast to 20 or 30 people in just a few moments. Perhaps there is even an app for this purpose.

Such digital communication technologies clearly make community building easier. Another example of the advantages of connecting digitally might be a chavruta, a pair of individuals who study text together every single week. With today's communications technology, if one of them must be out of town on the designated day, the study session can be conducted with any of a number of video-conferencing/calling programs. But in both of these examples, and many others like them, the use of digital communications is an ancillary aid to the face-to-face relationships of minyan or chavruta. I do not believe that they can substitute for such relationships entirely. They simply cannot replace the physically embodied presence that is so fundamental to community.

It is hardly original to claim that embodiment is a key element of Jewish communal culture or our basic humanity. Nevertheless, it is worth it at this point to review the notion briefly in order to emphasize the inadequacy of digital presence to substitute for actual presence. Here are just a few examples from Jewish ritual tradition that depend completely on our existence as beings with bodies. They require that we actually be present in the community.

- Baby boys are welcomed into the Jewish community at the age of eight days through ritual circumcision.
- Brides and grooms stand under a *chuppah*, an actual physical canopy symbolizing the home they will create together.
- A key element of the conversion ritual whereby a non-Jew becomes a Jew is the immersion of the entire body in a *mikveh*, or "ritual bath."
- One of the greatest mitzvot is the preparation of the body after death. Its importance can be judged by the fact that the volunteer community group that performs this sacred duty is called the *Chevra Kadisha*, or "Holy Society."
- One of the central mitzvot of the Passover seder is to eat the *matzah*, thereby literally tasting the memory of enslavement and redemption.
- Each weekday morning during the festival of Sukkot, tradition requires that we hold the lulav (a bouquet of palm, willow, and myrtle branches) and etrog (citron), recite a blessing, and shake them in all the directions of the compass.

It would be easy to multiply such examples. What they all share is that they are practices that are by definition fulfilled using our bodies. We hold, shake, smell, taste, and so on. There can be no virtual, electronic substitutes for such rituals. Furthermore, although a few of them can conceivably be performed in solitude (for example, one can shake the lulav and etrog on one's own), they are all typically performed in real community. So although I have performed a wedding that was streamed live on the Internet for the benefit of relatives who lived in Israel and could not make the long trip to the United States, and I myself have virtually "attended" the funeral of a dear friend by watching it streamed live when I was unable to fly to California to be there in person, the core of such sacred events must be constructed by real people sharing a real space. Such real connection is the essence of forming community, and thereby facilitating the emergence of God.

NOTES

1. Maimonides, *Mishneh Torah*, Hilkhot Tefilah 8:1.
2. Tractate Soferim 10:7.
3. Shulchan Arukh, Orach Chayim #55.
4. Babylonian Talmud, Sanhedrin 65b.
5. Gershon Scholem, "Golem." *Encyclopedia Judaica*, vol. 7, col. 755.
6. The question of whether machines with true artificial intelligence might ever be built in such an advanced and sophisticated way as to be truly conscious is a fascinating one. It is explored rather whimsically in a 2008 short story entitled "Article of Faith" by science fiction writer Mike Resnick. In the story, a robot janitor in a church comes to believe in God and Scripture and wishes to participate fully in the church service. The human members of the church are outraged. The story can be read online at http://www.baenebooks.com/chapters/1932093033/1932093033___1.htm
7. In the particular case of the golem, there is a fascinating side question about the golem's Jewish status. Not only must a minyan be comprised of ten conscious humans, but they must be Jewish. By what standards might the mystics have imagined the golem to be Jewish?
8. Maimonides, *Mishneh Torah*, Hilkhot Tefilah 8:3.
9. Babylonian Talmud, Berakhot 8a.
10. Babylonian Talmud, Berakhot 63b.
11. Babylonian Talmud, Shabbat 127a.
12. Pirkei Avot 5:25.
13. Tosefta Sanhedrin 11:6.
14. Abraham Isaac Kook, "Lights for Rebirth" in Arthur Hertzberg (ed.), *The Zionist Idea* (New York: Atheneum, 1973), 430.
15. Greenberg wonders, in a 2004 essay, if his thinking about holy secularity was perhaps profoundly influenced by the work of Christian theologians Dietrich Bonhoeffer and Harvey Cox. See Irving Greenberg, *For the Sake of Heaven and Earth* (Philadelphia: Jewish Publication Society, 2004), 28–29.
16. Mekhlita D'Rabbi Ishmael, Bahodesh section 5.
17. Sherry Turkle, *Alone Together: Why We Expect More from Technology and Less from Each Other* (New York: Basic Books, 2011), 155f.
18. The term "digital native" was coined by Mark Prensky in his 2001 article "Digital Natives, Digital Immigrants" as a label for those born in an era when digital communication was already quite common.
19. Turkle, *Alone Together*, 200.
20. *ibid.*, 233.
21. *ibid.*, 168.
22. This data was reported in an article by Bianca Bosker in *Huffington Post* on 11/19/2011 (http://www.huffingtonpost.com/2011/11/19/the-average-facebook-user_n_1102902.html—accessed July 30, 2013).
23. As reported in *Mail Online* on May 24, 2011, (http://www.dailymail.co.uk/sciencetech/article-1390266/Feeling-popular-The-average-22-year-old-1-000-plus-Facebook-friends-thats-50-times-parents.html—accessed July 30, 2013).
24. Turkle, *Alone Together*, 239.
25. Maimonides, *Mishneh Torah*, Hilkhot Tefilah 8:6–7.

26. http://oneshul.org/contact/—accessed August 1, 2013.

27. Michael Sabani, "In Defense of the Online Minyan." *Zeek*, December 3, 2012 (http://zeek.forward.com/articles/117182/—accessed August 1, 2013).

Chapter Seven

Exploring Loneliness

THE LONELY PROPHET

One of the saddest parts of the Torah for me is at the very end, the story of the death of Moses. It's not sad because Moses dies. We all die sooner or later and 120 is not a bad age to have reached. The death of Moses is sad because Moses dies alone and lonely. The first four verses of Deuteronomy 34 tell us that Moses ascended from the plains of Moab to the top of Mount Nebo, and there God showed him the promised land and told him that although this was in fact the land that God had promised to Abraham, Isaac, and Jacob, Moses could only look briefly at it from the mountaintop but would not be allowed to cross over into the land. Then we read: "Moses, the servant of the Eternal, died there in the land of Moab at the mouth of the Eternal. He buried him there in the valley in the land of Moab across from Beit Pe'or, and no person knows the place of his burial, until this very day."[1] It is quite clear from the text that no one was with Moses at the moment of his death—no one, that is, except God. The most common explanation of the text's explicit statement that no one knows where Moses is buried is that this narrative detail was an attempt to prevent Moses's burial place from becoming a shrine. In fact, many have commented on the repeated attempts in the stories about Moses to dissuade anyone from getting confused between Moses and God. Moses, the text wants us to believe, was "just" a man, a human leader, doing God's bidding. It was God who redeemed the Israelites from Egypt, led them through the wilderness, and gave them the Torah—not Moses. And although this may be part of the reason for the detailed description of the leader's death, I see in it something else.

From Moses's birth he is a lonely and solitary character. In early childhood his mother gives him up in order to protect him, and he spends his youth living in Pharaoh's household. But midrashic sources tell us what common sense already makes us suspect—that is, that he was not an altogether welcomed and beloved member of the household. There is a well-known story of baby Moses being tested by Pharaoh. The ruler, concerned that Moses would grow up to be an interloper, presents the baby with a plate of glowing coals and a plate of glittering gems. Like any baby, Moses is attracted to the sparkle of the gems and reaches for them; but an angel, knowing that this choice will lead to the baby's execution, swoops in and pushes his hand to touch the burning coals. The baby burns his fingers, sticks them in his mouth, and burns his tongue. The midrash functions as a just-so story to explain Moses's later speech impediment, but it is also an indication of Pharaoh's mistrust of this outsider. Unfortunately, however, the Hebrews also see Moses as an outsider, not really one of them. And this too makes sense, for Moses was raised in the heart of privileged Egyptian society while his "brethren" toiled as slaves. It is little wonder that when Moses intervenes in a quarrel between two Hebrews a day after killing an Egyptian taskmaster who was flogging a Hebrew slave, one of the two says, "Who made you an authority and judge over us? Do you intend to kill me the way you killed the Egyptian?"[2] Moses is not really accepted by his Egyptian foster family and not really accepted by the Hebrews either. He is a loner. He marries Zipporah and has two sons with her, but it seems that at some point early in the exodus story, she returns with her sons to her father's house in Midian.[3]

Indeed, the only one with whom Moses seems to spend any significant time is God. Between his forty days on the mountain with God and his frequent trips to the Tent of Meeting, he seems to be rather intimate with the divine presence. Thus it is hardly a surprise when Moses's life ends in isolation from all other people and he is accompanied up Mount Nebo only by God. God commands his death, although again the midrash picks up an important detail in the text quoted above. The text says that Moses died "at the *mouth* of the Eternal." Now the plain meaning of this strange phrase is clearly that it was at the *command*—that is, the *word*—of God. But in another famous midrash Moses is portrayed as objecting to impending death. God sends the angel of death to fetch Moses, but Moses finds one way after another to delay or deny the angel. Finally, God realizes that He must personally take Moses's life and so He takes his soul with a kiss. On the one hand this is a tender and poignant image, but on the other we get the sense that Moses got more kisses from God than he ever got from any humans. Moses lived in solitude, separated from humankind, and thus he died as well—accompanied and comforted only by God.

Now compare this image with those of Sarah and Jacob, whose deaths I find much less sad. In Genesis 23 Sarah dies and Abraham seems to kneel or sit beside her, for the text tells us that "Abraham got up from beside his dead and spoke to the Hittites"[4] to negotiate the purchase of a burial site for his beloved wife. And in Genesis 49, as Jacob is about to die, he gathers all his sons around him and gives each of them a blessing, even though they had caused him great suffering earlier on by making him believe that Joseph was dead. In both these cases, and in others as well, the protagonist dies in the company of loved ones. But Moses dies as he lived, alone.

For me Moses's solitude makes him a tragic figure, for the companionship of God is not enough for a human being. God Himself admits that this is so. After we read repeatedly in the first chapter of Genesis that God created one thing after another and declared that each was *good*, and then that the whole creation was *very good*, we are somewhat startled in the second chapter when verse 18 starts out, "Eternal God said, 'It is *not* good . . .'" What could possibly be not good in this newly created world? How could it be? The verse continues, ". . . for the human to be alone.'" This comes as a bit of a shock. For centuries we have lived with a common notion of God's omniscience, but suddenly—just after the creation of the world—it seems that God has made an error. If God had believed all along that "it is not good for the human to be alone," why did He create Adam alone? My own midrashic speculation on this question leads me to conclude that God did not think He was creating the human alone. Rather, God imagined that He and the human creature would be friends, partners, companions. It was only after observing the man in the garden for a while (how long it took we cannot say) that God realized His own companionship was insufficient for the man. Despite God's constant presence, the man still seemed lonely. That this was God's miscalculation can be learned from the way God analyzes the problem. After noting that it is not good for the human to be alone, God continues, "I shall make for him an *ezer k'negdo*." Now this unusual phrase is not easy to understand with precision. The Jewish Publication Society translation renders it "a fitting helper," the New Revised Standard Version renders it "a helper who is just right for him," the New International Version uses "a helper suitable for him," and Everett Fox decides on "a helper corresponding to him." Although these translations all agree that *ezer* means "helper," they differ a bit from one another on the meaning of the word *k'negdo*. Whether it means "fitting" or "just right" or "suitable" or "corresponding," apparently it describes something that God cannot be. Interestingly, it also describes something animals cannot be, as we see in the next scene where God creates all the animals and has the man name them in an attempt—what turns out to be a futile attempt—to find an ezer k'negdo. Only one of his own kind, another human, can relieve the man's loneliness. This is why I find Moses tragic. For some reason he never learns the lesson that both God and Adam learn in the early days of the Garden of Eden. Perhaps he does not know how to connect with other people, or perhaps the disruptions of his childhood, where he was handed back and forth between his mother and his foster mother, scarred him emotionally. Whatever the reason may be, Moses lives and dies alone, finding companionship only with God.

A BRIEF TASTE OF LONELINESS

Many years ago I was scheduled to be a scholar-in-residence for a New England group at a camp over Shabbat. As the weekend drew near and we discussed logistics, it turned out that the group would spend Friday evening in its home synagogue (an hour or so from the camp) and would come to the camp on Saturday morning. I explained that it was not my practice to travel on Shabbat and the organizers assured me that this was not a problem. I could arrive at the camp on Friday before sundown and they would arrange in advance for the camp caretaker to have my room ready and to supply food, wine, candles, and anything else I needed. I got to the camp and shortly before sundown I lit my Shabbat candles. Alone. A bit later I sat down to recite kiddush over a glass of wine. Alone. I recited the blessing over two lovely challahs. Alone. And I ate a perfectly nice Shabbat dinner. Alone. In the years since then, I have remembered that Shabbat as the most dismal, lonely, painful Shabbat of my life. It taught me that Shabbat—and other Jewish celebrations as well—are experiences that can only be relished with others. Whether the "others" are one's family, or a group of friends, or colleagues, is almost irrelevant, as long as the moments of ritual and observance are shared in community. This life in community, as I pointed out earlier, is the very essence of Jewish experience. If the greatest mitzvah is any observance that creates community, then loneliness is the state of human existence that presents the greatest impediment to the mitzvah.

From a historical perspective, it is significant that there has never been a large-scale movement in Judaism that encourages individual seclusion as a path to spiritual uplift. Where such encouragement is found, it is generally noted as a practice of a very few individuals whose intimacy with God was seen as exemplary, but it is almost never prescribed as normative for the community at large. The sole exception to this generalization seems to come in the teachings of Rabbi Nachman of Bratslav (d. 1810), the great-grandson of the Baal Shem Tov, the founder of modern Hasidism. Rabbi Nachman taught as follows: "*Hitboddedut* [seclusion] is a supreme activity, greater than any other. One should fix for oneself an hour or more to go off alone, in a room or out in the field, to converse with one's Maker, with complaints, words of love and supplication, to plead and beg that God bring one closer to God, and to God's service, in truth."[5] But even here the prescription is that one seclude oneself in order to converse with God only for an hour or so each day. The rest of the time one is to live, study, and especially pray in community.

These observations make sense in light of the model I have proposed whereby God's consciousness is seen as an emergent property resulting from the interaction of a vast multitude of human consciousnesses. The model suggests that it is very difficult, perhaps virtually impossible, to interact with God without the presence of an interactive community.

WHAT ABOUT *THE LONELY MAN OF FAITH*?

This model of the emergence of God's consciousness fits well with the preponderance of postbiblical Jewish tradition regarding the connections between human beings and God. Throughout the Bible there are numerous reports of individuals who have intimate personal relationships with God. Abraham, Jacob, Moses, and most of the prophets communicate directly with God on a regular basis, and He communicates with them as well. But as we have seen, as Rabbinic Judaism began to emerge in the postbiblical era, such personal encounters with the divine became increasingly rare and were replaced with communal interaction with God, typically occurring in prayer and study. From the end of the biblical era to our own day, the direct, individual experience of God has generally been relegated to the rare kabbalist, the mystic for whom the communal experience of God in the deconstruction of a page of Talmud or the raised voices of a minyan at prayer are not sufficient. But such individuals almost always constituted a minority of the Jewish people,[6] while the majority—if they had the experience of encountering God at all—did so through the more mainstream modalities of community study and prayer.

In light of this historical tendency, it is both surprising and perplexing to read *The Lonely Man of Faith,* a seminal and well-known monograph by the eminent philosopher Rabbi Joseph B. Soloveitchik. This extended essay, first published in *Tradition* magazine in 1965, is rooted in the author's distinction between the portrayal of Adam in the first chapter of Genesis (Soloveitchik calls him Adam the first) and the portrayal in the second chapter (Adam the second). By way of brief summary, Adam the first is a utilitarian builder, a fixer, dedicated to improving his own (and the world's) dignity by creating new and better technologies, thereby fulfilling the mandate given him and his female partner (who is created together with him) by God to "Be fruitful and multiply, fill up the earth and conquer/master it."[7] The question that drives him is "How does the cosmos function?"[8] Adam the first is by nature a social being but his relationships are utilitarian. He lives in community because doing so makes his work easier, more efficient, and more effective, not because he has any deep existential or spiritual need for companionship. Adam the second is a very different creature and asks very different questions:

> Why did the world ... come into existence? ... What is the message that is embedded in ... matter and what does the great challenge reaching me from beyond the fringes of the universe as well as from the depths of my tormented soul mean? ... Who is He who trails me steadily ... like an everlasting shadow, and vanishes into the recesses of transcendence the very instant I turn around to confront this numinous, awesome, and mysterious "He"? ... Who is He to whom Adam clings in passionate, all-consuming love and from whom he flees in mortal fear and dread?[9]

Adam the second goes about answering these questions in a very different way from that of Adam the first. I find Soloveitchik's explanation deeply poetic and moving:

> Adam the second explores not the scientific abstract universe but the irresistibly fascinating qualitative world where he establishes an intimate relation with God. The Biblical metaphor referring to God breathing life into Adam alludes to the actual preoccupation of the latter with God, to his genuine living experience of God. ... [He] lives in close union with God. His existential "I" experience is interwoven in the awareness of communing with the Great Self whose footprints he discovers along the many tortuous paths of creation.[10]

Adam the second is the man of faith. After being formed out of the dust of the earth, he has had life breathed into him by God, an act that resonates with physicality, intimacy, and love. Two images come immediately to mind. The first is the "rescue breathing" part of CPR (cardiopulmonary resuscitation). A typical "how-to" website describes the procedure as follows: "Tilt the head back and lift the chin. Pinch nose and cover the mouth with yours and blow until you see the chest rise."[11] This is literally the giving of life. But the other image is that of the passionate, deep, mouth-to-mouth kisses of lovers.

And so Adam the second has been given life and loved by God, and the experience has left him eternally longing for more. One gets the sense from reading Soloveitchik's words, which are at times suffused with a deep anguish, that Adam the second—having tasted the love of God—abandons his interest in all other pursuits, especially worldly pursuits, to focus on his lifelong search for more and more moments of divine encounter. For him "[t]o be means to be the only one, singular and different, and consequently lonely. For what causes man to be lonely ... if not the awareness of his uniqueness and exclusiveness? The 'I' is lonely ... because there is no one who exists like the 'I.'"[12] In terms of human companionship, Adam the second can only be satisfied with what Soloveitchik calls either the "faith community" or the "covenantal community." Unlike the utilitarian communities that Adam the first naturally and easily forms, the covenantal community of Adam the second always consists of three partners: "I, thou, and He."[13] Lest there be any doubt in our minds as to what he means by "He," Soloveitchik adds "the He in whom all being is rooted and in whom everything finds its rehabilitation and, consequently, redemption."[14] God's role in the covenantal community is the sine qua non for that community's existence. And even when Adam the second finds himself in a covenantal community (for example, a prayer community), we get the distinct impression that it is God's presence—rather than that of the other nine worshipers who constitute the minyan—that Adam cherishes.

How different might the life of the person of faith be if he or she were to embrace the notion of God's Self, which Soloveitchik at one point refers to as the "Great True Real Self,"[15] as the emergent property of the vast and complex interactions of and interconnectedness among billions of conscious human selves? First of all, the stark distinction that Soloveitchik makes between Adam the first and Adam the second, especially with regard to how the two of them view the cosmos, might turn out to be a bit of a false dichotomy. Adam the first is described as entering into social relationships, forming communities, for utilitarian purposes. His community is "forged by the indomitable desire for success and triumph and consist[s] at all times of two grammatical *personae*, the 'I' and the 'thou' who collaborate in order to fulfill their interests."[16] This description sounds mildly disparaging, as if collaborating in order to fulfill common interests is somehow a rather shallow and philosophically/ontologically flimsy basis for a community. It might just as well have added the word "merely" after "collaborate": Adam the first collaborates with his neighbors *merely* to fulfill their common interests. But to place—or even to imply—such a valence on fulfilling common interests is, I would argue, foreign to the spirit of Judaism. In the centuries after what was perceived as the end of prophecy (i.e, the end of direct communication from God to human beings), Judaism focused increasingly on a system of behaviors, mitzvot, and halakhot that would sketch the boundaries of Jewish life and sacred experience. The ingenuity of this innovative system lay precisely in its *lack* of focus on the individual's personal, face-to-face encounter with God. Instead the content is altogether normal and everyday, as we are about to see.

PIN THE TAIL ON THE TALMUD

Here's a simple game that anyone can play. It's sort of a variation on that old birthday party standard, Pin the Tail on the Donkey, but with the Talmud (in the original or in English translation) standing in for the donkey. As I write this, I'll play just to demonstrate how it goes.

I reach out to the shelf on which my many volumes of Talmud sit and select one at random, without looking. Then I open it to a page, again at random. Let's see what I find. It turns out that I've opened Tractate Megillah and find myself on page 29a: "One may suspend the study of Torah for taking out a dead body [for burial] and for bringing in a bride [to the wedding canopy]." I'll play the game once more. This time I've grabbed Tractate Baba Batra and opened it to page 93a. The top of the page drops me into the middle of a sentence—not so useful, so I go to the middle of the second line on the page to find the start of a sentence, and here we are: "Come and hear: If an ox gored a cow and her [dead] fetus is found at her side, and it is unknown whether she gave birth before he gored or after he gored, [the owner of the ox] pays half-damage for the cow and one-quarter-damage for the fetus."

I find this a fascinating game, have played it often, and strongly recommend that you try it. The results almost never vary. The issues I find by randomly selecting a page from a randomly selected volume of the Talmud are inevitably related to elements of creating, or maintaining, or conducting the affairs of a community. It might be a community of two—say, a married or betrothed couple if I have randomly selected Tractate Ketubot (i.e., wedding contracts) or Tractate Kiddushin (i.e., betrothals)—or it might be a much larger community, as in the two examples here. These are, to use Soloveitchik's language, the sorts of issues that concern Adam the first, who constructs community in order to make sure enough people are available to bury the dead, or escort brides to their wedding canopies, or to fix monetary compensation in a fair manner when one member of the society has harmed another. They are the concerns of a group that is seeking to serve its common interests. But very rarely does the randomly selected text deal with an individual's longing for or conversations with God, these being Adam the second's typical concerns. But if we think of God's conscious self as emergent, then the discussion of whether or not to suspend our study of the Torah to attend to the needs of the dead, or the discussion of how to set compensation for damage that may or may not have been caused by a particular ox, are no longer simply utilitarian issues. Because they entail questions of interaction with other members of the community, they are encounters with God. This shift in perspective may teach Adam the second something important about human relationships. When God breathes life into Adam's nostrils in a deeply intimate gesture of love, Adam is so overwhelmed by the experience that he commits his life to recapturing it. When he cannot do so, he feels abandoned and lonely. The situation is reminiscent of young lovers who are absolutely besotted with one another. Merely seeing each other from across the room, much less embracing one another, makes their hearts beat faster and their faces flush with passion. It is a glorious state of human existence. But then the lovers marry and sooner or later their relationship changes. Often interactions between the spouses concern the building and maintenance of a household. Paying rent, buying groceries, and deciding when it's time to move to a bigger place are the sorts of ordinary matters that the couple's conversations address. And they mourn, for they remember the days of new love, of increased heart rate and flushed skin.

This is not a new observation. It has been made in countless therapists' offices for the benefit of countless confused and lonely couples. And the solution to the problem, the real long-term solution, is not to go on a romantic weekend getaway, though such mini-vacations are delightful. The solution is to recognize the love, intimacy, and commitment reflected in a discussion of whether the budget can handle the needed repainting of the porch or whether both of us must go to Tuesday's parent-teacher conference. The intimacy and love in these interactions is subtle, so very subtle that we often miss it altogether. Adam the second is lonely because he mistakes the oh-so-subtle intimacy of interactions with God's Great True Real Self for a total lack of intimacy. So enthralled was he with God's creation-moment kiss that he cannot bear to have banal relationships, utilitarian relationships, with God or with his fellow human beings. He can't bear to study Talmud in chavruta or to sit on the synagogue's Building and Grounds Committee because God's presence in such mundane activities is just too thin.

Perhaps this was Moses's situation as well. Both the biblical narrative and the midrashic expansion of that narrative portray Moses as being special, even extraordinary, from birth. In a time when the Egyptians had promulgated a murderous decree against all Hebrew baby boys, Moses's mother saw "how beautiful he was" and "hid him for three months."[17] In a typical midrash, we find the event described thus: "At the moment of Moses's birth, the entire world was filled with light. In this text it is written '. . . she saw that he was good [*ki tov*], and in another text it is written 'and God saw the light, that it was good [*ki tov*].'"[18] Here the sublime glory of the baby Moses is compared with the glory of the world's creation. Moses's special status is reaffirmed when he is brought into Pharaoh's household as a foster child, beloved by Pharaoh's daughter. And then, in Exodus 3 and 4, Moses has his first personal encounter with God at the burning bush. The encounter is unprecedented in its intimacy, as God points out by hinting at the most personal divine name. When Moses asks what he should tell the skeptical Hebrews when they ask the name of this God who sent him to free them, God identifies Himself as *Ehyeh Asher Ehyeh.*[19]

This enigmatic identification, which may be translated as "I am what I am," or perhaps "I will be what I will be," contains a foreshadowing of God's explicit revelation to Moses just a few chapters later. In what seems like a retelling of the interaction at the burning bush, God says to Moses, "I am *YHWH*. I appeared to Abraham, to Isaac, and to Jacob as *El Shaddai*, but [by] My Name *YHWH* I was not known to them."[20] This revelation by God of His most personal name puts Moses in a position of intimacy and closeness with God that has perhaps been unknown since God breathed/kissed life into Adam the second. Even Abraham, God's chosen covenantal partner, was not granted this degree of intimacy, at least according to God's recollection of the relationship as reported here to Moses.

Given this early experience, it is not so surprising to see Moses spend forty days on the mountain alone with God, or to see them together in the Tent of Meeting on a regular basis, with no one else ever allowed into those meetings. And given these many private, intimate encounters, it is also not surprising that Moses had little use for the banalities of common social interactions. Once God has revealed His innermost Self to you, it must be extremely difficult to put up with ordinary human conversations, even important ones. And thus it is little wonder that Moses's life was ended by the mouth of God, with a divine kiss, the way Adam the second's life was started, and that this very intimate moment was witnessed by no other human being. In fact, whereas Adam the second lives a life of loneliness after just one brief, initial contact from God, Moses is all the lonelier, for the last third of his life (from the age of 80, when he encountered God at the burning bush, until his death at 120) was peppered with numerous moments of private divine tenderness. In fact, the Torah's final analysis of the man rings so very true: "And never again has there arisen in Israel a prophet like Moses whom The Eternal knew face to face."[21]

THE LONELY PROPHET IS NOT A ROLE MODEL

The reality of Jewish life, however, since its early development in the Talmudic period, never set up either Adam the second or Moses as a role model to be emulated in day-to-day behavior by ordinary Jews. Instead the most normative model became the rabbi, a scholar/teacher/student whose life was lived always in community and whose prestige was often measured by the number of his students. That this is so can be seen in two specific examples. The first concerns the greatness of the second century CE sage Rabbi Akiva ben Joseph, whom the Talmud somewhat ironically portrays as being almost as great as Moses. The Talmud reports that he had 24,000 students.[22] And even if this number is not precise or historically trustworthy, it suggests that Akiva was remembered for, among other things, the tremendous size of the community of learning that he created. It is precisely his role as the center of a large community that gives him his status.

The second example comes from Jewish burial and mourning practices. It is well known that Jewish law requires that a dead body be buried as soon after death as possible. However, the burial may be postponed if doing so will enhance *k'vod ha-met*, the honor and dignity given to the dead. And one well-known reason to delay for the sake of k'vod ha-met is the case of a great sage who has had many disciples whose presence at the funeral will increase the honor shown to the dead person. If, as is not uncommon, these disciples are scattered all over the world, a funeral may be postponed for a day or two to give the grieving students the time needed to arrive at the site of their beloved teacher's burial. The point of both of these examples is that a rabbi is first and foremost a teacher, and a teacher is only a teacher in the context of his or her students and their relationship with the teacher. The solitary mystic or reclusive scholar who spends most of his time in lonely spiritual pursuits has rarely been held up as a model in Judaism. In fact, in a flourish of revisionist recollection, the rabbis of the Talmud dub Moses *Moshe Rabenu* "Moses our Teacher/Rabbi," thereby (mis-)remembering him not as the lonely man of faith who was accompanied—both in life and in death—primarily by God, but as the quintessential rabbinic teacher of students.

A NEW TWIST ON *AL TIFROSH*

One of the most quoted maxims of Rabbinic literature is the warning attributed to Hillel in Pirkei Avot 2:5, "*Al tifrosh min ha-tzibbur* [Do not separate from the community]." This teaching is usually employed in attempts to encourage participation in communal organizations and events, or to discourage splinter groups or rebellious moves by individuals in the Jewish community. But now, taking into account all that I have written here, I want to propose a deeper, more theological reading of the implications of this beloved statement: Do not separate from the community, because it is only in the midst of community, in the discussing, arguing, listening, negotiating, and debating that happens when human beings come together to form community, that God emerges. Loneliness and the life of covenant are simply incompatible.

NOTES

1. Deut. 34:5–6.
2. Ex. 2:14.
3. Zipporah's departure is never explicitly mentioned, but in Exodus 18:2 Jethro brings her back to Moses with her sons. The text describes Moses's warm welcome of his father-in-law but says not a word about how he reacted to the return of Zipporah or their sons, and Zipporah is barely mentioned in the rest of the Torah. Thus, whether she returned home with Jethro after a brief visit or whether she remained with the Israelites in their journeys, there certainly seems to be no closeness between her and her husband.
4. Gen. 23:3.
5. *Likutei Moharan* II:25.
6. The one notable exception to this statement came in the late 18th and early 19th century when Hasidism captured the imagination of a large number of Eastern European Jews. Even during this period, however, I suspect that the close, personal, direct relationships with God were characteristic of the *tzaddikim*, or charismatic individual community leaders, and were much less frequently a part of the everyday spiritual life of the average Hasid. An illustration of the ordinary nature of the Hasid's everyday life may be seen in the story told of Rabbi Levi Yitzchak of Berditchev, who one morning came across a man wearing *tallit* and *tefillin* (prayer

shawl and phylacteries) while greasing the wheels of his wagon. Instead of scolding the man for wearing garments of prayer while doing such dirty work, the rabbi exclaimed "Dear God! Look how pious Your people are! Even when they grease their wagon wheels they contemplate Your Name!" The story is found in Martin Buber, *Tales of the Hasidim: Early Masters* (New York, Schocken Books: 1972), 222.

7. Gen. 1:28.
8. Joseph B Soloveitchik, *The Lonely Man of Faith*. (Lanham, MD, and New York: Jason Aronson/Rowman and Littlefield: 2004), 13.
9. *ibid.* 21–22.
10. *ibid.* 23–24.
11. https://depts.washington.edu/learncpr/quickcpr.html. Accessed 7/2/2014.
12. Soloveitchik, *Lonely Man of Faith*, 40–41.
13. Note that Soloveitchik is *not* using the words "I" and "thou" in a Buberian sense, nor does he seem to have any intention to reference Martin Buber's dialogic philosophy.
14. Soloveitchik, *Lonely Man of Faith*, 43.
15. *ibid,* 79.
16. *ibid,* 43.
17. Ex. 2:2.
18. *Yalkut Shimoni* #166 on Exodus 2.
19. Ex. 3:14.
20. Ex. 6:2–3.
21. Deut. 33:10.
22. Babylonian Talmud, Yevamot 62b. Note that the text does not say "twenty-four thousand," but rather, "twelve thousand pairs of students." This reflects, once again, the necessity of studying with a *chavruta* rather than by one's self.

Epilogue

A Brief, Final Thought: But What If I'm Wrong?

This book has made one simple proposal, based on one simple premise. The premise is that the human conscious mind, that which each of us experiences as *I*, is the emergent result of the hugely complex interactions among the vast number of neurons in our brain. The proposal based on this premise is that the mind of God (that is, the extent to which it makes any sense for us to think of God as being a sentient Self) is the emergent result of the hugely complex interactions among the vast number of human (and perhaps nonhuman) consciousnesses that populate our planet (and perhaps other planets in far distant corners of the universe).

But what if the premise turns out to be wrong? As I observed earlier, the scientific explanation of human consciousness is in its infancy and there is nothing even vaguely resembling consensus among cognitive scientists on where it comes from or how it works. Although the emergence model that I have described here makes a tremendous amount of sense to me, I am willing to admit that in twenty or fifty or a hundred years this model for understanding human consciousness may have long since been relegated to the dustbin of history. If this were to happen, would the ideas, proposals, and questions that I have discussed in these pages become completely irrelevant and pointless?

I think not. And here is why: Contemporary Judaism suffers—among other reasons—because many (perhaps most) of today's Jews, having been well educated in an open, pluralistic, and highly scientific culture,[1] don't take belief in God very seriously. God exists in their vocabularies, so they may use an expression like "Thank God!" after hearing that a friend or relative survived a traffic accident unhurt, but I think that deep down they don't really believe that God was the reason for the escape from injury. Likewise, they may occasionally go to synagogue and participate in worship services, but I don't think that they believe deep down that there's a Someone Up There who is listening and caring. For many—or most—it's simply a comforting exercise in community togetherness. That's my impression of contemporary American Jews.

I believe it is very important that we begin to discuss these ideas and beliefs. Plato taught that "the unexamined life is not worth living."[2] I would modify this just a bit and claim that the unexamined religious life is not worth living. For if we live our religious lives without thought, without questioning, without an honest examination of what we believe and why, we end up turning a rich heritage of mind and soul into a dry, two-dimensional set of meaningless rituals with no symbolic value. Such a religious life has little appeal for me, and I suggest that it has little appeal for most thoughtful contemporary Jews.

I recently spent several hours speaking with a very bright woman, well on her way to earning a Ph.D., who was raised in a nominally Protestant environment and now, in her late thirties, wants to explore converting to Judaism. We studied the first four chapters of Genesis together. We got to Genesis 1:26, "Let us make *Adam* in our image," and she stopped, perplexed. Why the use of the plural pronouns "us/our"? I explored several possible explanations of the strange usage with her, including (a) God is using the royal we; (b) God is speaking to all the other creations He has made in the previous six days; (c) God is speaking with angels; (d) the male and female aspects of God are speaking with one another. My student was somewhat startled by both the number of possibilities (these four obviously do not exhaust the entire range of possibilities) and my openness to entertaining all sorts of strange questions and ideas about God. She had grown up with a vague and limited set of axioms about God and had always thought that these axioms were not up for question or discussion. What she realized as we went through the text, line by line, was that it is completely permissible—at least according to my sense of Jewish tradition—to ask challenging questions and suggest unconventional answers. If study is to be personally meaningful, we are obligated to ask such questions and suggest such answers.

If we are to take the religious aspects of Judaism seriously, we must give ourselves complete permission to question boldly and think creatively and imaginatively about our beliefs, especially our beliefs about God. If we go along quietly, tacitly accepting the old, worn theological axioms we heard in childhood that we no longer believe (if we ever did) but that we feel incapable or uncomfortable overturning, then our religious and spiritual lives will become ever more meaningless. We must allow ourselves the freedom to ask hard questions. What kind of God do I *really* believe in? Is the Sunday School image of God (old man, long beard, stern judge, loving parent, etc.)

the only option, such that if I do not accept it I must declare myself an atheist or an agnostic? How can I imagine God having a role in my life? How can I *not* lie to myself about my beliefs?

Although at this moment I am firmly committed to the model I have proposed in these pages, it may turn out someday that the model makes no sense. If this should happen, then at least the freedom I have explored here to ask—and suggest radically new answers to—these kinds of questions will stand as a model for others. These are the questions we should be asking. Whether you end up agreeing with my answers or not is almost beside the point, for the most important thing is to learn how to ask the questions. That is what I hope to have demonstrated here.

NOTES

1. I do not intend to suggest that many, or most, people think scientifically in any serious way. Rather, contemporary American Jews have been brought up in an environment in which testable, empirically verifiable, logical things are believable, and things that cannot (or have not been) tested or verified are less believable, or unbelievable. One need only recall the number of television commercials in the last fifty years that have featured a serious-looking gentleman in a white lab coat (who was never identified per se as a scientist or a physician, but the lab coat did plant the suggestion in our minds!) touting the wonders of a product, to see the influence of science on our culture.

2. Plato, *Apology* section 38a.